Grieving the Loss of Your Horse:
How to Survive Your Journey

#Nuzzles ♡

Grieving the Loss of Your Horse:

How to Survive Your Journey

Revised and Expanded Second Edition

Rebecca M. Crow, BS, CAPLC

Grieving the Loss of Your Horse:

How to Survive Your Journey

Revised and Expanded
Second Edition

ISBN-13: 978-1-976-38963-4 Paperback
ISBN-10: 1976389631 e-book
Published through Kindle

Cover Photograph by Kenny Webster on Unsplash.com
Find more information about
Kenny Webster Photography
kennywebsterphotos.com

NOTE

THE STORIES IN THIS BOOK ARE BASED ON WHAT HAPPENED TO REAL PEOPLE. NAMES OF PERSONS, LOCATIONS, BUSINESSES AND MANY OTHER DETAILS HAVE BEEN CHANGED OR ADDED TO DISGUISE IDENTITIES. MANY OF THESE STORIES ARE COMPOSITES OF MORE THAN ONE PERSON OR FAMILY'S EXPERIENCE IN LOSING A DEARLY LOVED HORSE.

DISCLAIMER

THIS BOOK IS NOT INTENDED TO GIVE OR REPLACE ANY PROFESSIONAL VETERINARY, FARRIER, FINANCIAL OR LEGAL ADVICE. THE AUTHOR IS NEITHER A VETERINARIAN, NOR A FARRIER, NOR A FINANCIAL PROFESSIONAL, NOR AN ATTORNEY. IF YOU FIND YOURSELF AND YOUR HORSE IN ANY SITUATION SIMILAR TO THOSE DESCRIBED IN THIS BOOK CONSULT YOUR OWN VETERINARIAN, FARRIER, ATTORNEY OR OTHER PROFESSIONAL.

Dedication

This book is dedicated to my parents Larry and Joy Meeks, who allowed and encouraged me to adopt and love animals, starting with tiny ones like goldfish and advancing to larger ones including dogs and horses as I grew up.

CONTENTS

CHAPTER ONE

Introduction

The experience of going through grieving the loss of your horse due to illness, accident, natural disaster, fire, theft, old age or other causes can be a long and painful process. You have developed a treasured relationship with your horse and the season of your life that you shared with him is still very important to you. Horses can live 25 to thirty or even more years. Your relationship with your horse may last decades. Losing a horse you have loved for years can hurt more than you can stand. It can be a crushing blow to your heart.

Of course horses can die at any age, and losing a young one can hurt just as badly as losing an elderly horse that has lived a good long life in your care. You may lose a horse you have only had for a few months or years. You may fall in love and create a strong bond with your horse quite soon after you buy him. And no matter how long you have had your horse it hurts to lose him.

Some foals die before or shortly after birth due to many different reasons such as birth defects and illness or even the death of the mare. This can destroy your dreams of a long anticipated newborn. It can hurt just as much as losing a horse you have had for a while.

You may find yourself in a situation where you feel that your horse is in such bad health or so badly injured that having your veterinarian put her down is the best choice you can make to stop her suffering. And since you do spend a lot of hours every week with your horse, trail riding, showing, grooming, practicing for competition, feeding, hand grazing and other activities, it may take a long time to process losing him.

There is no set time limit when you should be finished with grieving because each horse owner, each horse and each set of circumstances is different. So give yourself all of the time you need. And it is possible that you may feel that loss deeply for the rest of your life. It is your experience that nobody else can fully understand no matter how much they care about you and your horse. And you are entitled to your own feelings.

Selling your horse can also trigger the grieving process. It may be time to move on to a more challenging mount or time to choose a younger one to ride in shows. Like so many of us, you may be having financial difficulties forcing a sale. You may be going away to college or entering a new marriage, need more time for your family or going through a divorce. You may even want to sell because your interests have changed to other goals, desires and accomplishments. You may have suffered an injury or illness and can no longer ride or take care of your horse.

Retiring your horse on your own farm or just keeping her to ride for recreation may or may not be an option for you, due to time, finances or space to keep her along with your new horse. These reasons can also cause you to grieve losing your relationship with that special horse.

And sure, one way or another you can always get another horse eventually but that may not diminish your pain and sadness of losing the one you already had. Thinking about that too soon can sometimes make grieving even more painful. You may need to give yourself time and permission to grieve without feeling the rush to replace her. Your replacement will be a good horse but may not have some of the same special qualities and funny little quirks that touched your heart or made you laugh. So you may not feel that you are ready to bond with him if it is too soon after your horse's death or sale.

You may already have another horse who was good friends with the horse you lost. Horses are social animals that have feelings too and may suffer from the loss of your other horse, especially if you only had two horses in your herd anyway. (And in lager herds horses tend to pair with a special buddy.) In that case you may need to consider getting another horse right away as a companion horse for him to alleviate his anxiety. There are options for that even if you are not ready to make a long term commitment to a new horse. You can temporarily foster a horse from a sanctuary farm that rescues horses. You can borrow a horse from a friend or family member. You can even get a companion goat or other animal for him until you are ready to get another horse.

And in the case of either the death or sale of your horse, there is some evidence that horses go to Heaven. So you may be reunited with her again someday. We will explore the experience of grieving and the possibility that you will again have a future together in Heaven. Both issues can be very important to those suffering through the loss of their horses.

The following chapters contain stories about people who have lost their horses under different circumstances. The stories illustrate how different people react in different ways under different circumstances and how they handled it. No two people will grieve in the same way or for the same amount of time. You may find your own story in this book. You may also find the stories of other people you know who have lost their own horses. Use the stories to help yourself through grieving, as well as your family and friends who have lost their own horses. You are not alone in this experience. A lot of horse people have been there and understand your pain.

CHAPTER 2

THE PHASES OF GRIEVING THE LOSS OF YOUR HORSE

There are several phases of grieving according to a lot of experts in this field of study. These phases may apply to any situation where there is a heart breaking loss, most particularly to losing people and animals you have loved. The following is an overview of the phases of grieving the loss of your horse.

The Phases of Grieving the Loss of Your Horse:

1.   The initial shock that your horse is gone

2.   Feelings of anger and outrage at losing your horse

3.   Wishful thinking about somehow getting your horse back safe and sound

4.   Feeling sad about losing your horse

5.   Finally coming to grips with the reality of your horse's death, sale or theft.

Phase One: The Initial Shock that Your Horse is Gone

First comes the initial shock and disbelief, when you think the death of your horse is not real. You may think, how could this possibly happen to me? It could not be real, could it? Your mind may generate other possible reasons for your horse not being there when you walk into the barn. You still want to think of your horse as living in the present time. Maybe your horse has just wandered off into the neighbor's field and will come home soon. Or maybe someone else borrowed him to ride and has not come back yet. Surely it is all a colossal mistake to think he is really gone for good. There must be some logical reason other than death. There has to be. It is just too hard to believe!

Phase Two: Feelings of Outrage at Losing Your Horse

Then come the feelings of outrage and wondering why this is happening to you. You may feel angry at yourself or another person or God for causing your horse's death. Your mind goes through a bunch of "if only" thoughts and feelings over and over again. If only you had not gone out to dinner or on vacation; if only you had checked on her one more time the night she died; if only you had not ridden so hard that day; if only the veterinarian had gotten there sooner; if only the farrier had seen the signs; if only the barn manager had paid closer attention; if only you were a better person it would not have happened to you. Other similar thoughts may race relentlessly through your mind.

And there is a strong likelihood that none of those things had anything to do with the reasons or cause of death. You are just angry at this point and may desperately want somewhere to place the blame, especially on yourself.

Phase Three: Wishful Thinking About Somehow Getting Your Horse Back Safe and Sound

After the outrage comes wishful thinking, when you vow to be a better person if your horse's death can somehow be reversed and you could find her happily munching on grass in her favorite spot in the pasture. You may want to make a deal with God that if He will give your horse back to you, you will be a kinder person, volunteer at a local non-profit organization or donate money to a worthy cause if only He will bring your horse back.

Phase Four: Feeling Sad About Losing Your Horse

Then sadness sets in as you begin to realize that there is nothing you can do to change the circumstances and you feel helpless. You cannot reverse it. There is nothing you can do to change it. This sadness may last a long time and you feel like you are swimming in a sea of raw emotions. Or in some cases those intense feelings may pass relatively soon. It is different for each person going through it. Your pain is your pain.

Phase Five: Finally Coming to Grips with the Reality of Your Horse's Death

After the sadness has been there for a while you come to grips with the reality of your horse's death when you have worked through a lot of the pain and are slowly realizing that you will go on with your life without your much loved friend. That does not mean you will forget your horse or dishonor her memory. It does not mean you will never feel pain and sadness again about losing him. It just means you accept the new reality of living without your special horse with all of the up and down feelings that go along with getting back to a more normal routine in your daily life.

These feelings may come back at other times in your life

People often find themselves cycling through the grieving process multiple times as life goes on. Other losses can bring back memories and feelings of grieving the loss of your horse again such as the death of another animal or even a person in your life who may have also shared your love for your horse. You may find yourself stumbling across your horse's halter, blanket, a picture or show ribbons and trophies you won together and those things can trigger these emotions again. It is normal for that to happen.

You will get through those moments and find comfort in your own time and in your own way. Be patient with yourself.

CHAPTER 3

YOU CAN GRIEVE LOSING YOUR HORSE DURING DIFFERENT CIRCUMSTANCES

Grieving the loss of your horse through trauma or illness

Losing a horse to death under any circumstances can be heartbreaking. Losing a horse through illness, accident, natural disaster, or in an unexpected fire can be a devastating trauma.

However it happens, you are likely to go through a process of grieving that could take some time.

Veronica's Story (Part One)

Veronica and her family lived on a working farm on the outskirts of a small town in Missouri. She was a student at the local community college still living at home to help out with the family business and enjoy the freedom of riding her horse every day. She could not stand the thought of living in a crowded dorm far from her family home and her mare Lucy.

While eating an early supper during one evening of particularly bad thunderstorms her family heard the screaming sound of the siren used to warn that tornadoes were in the area. Veronica and her parents Kevin and Sharon ran to the basement of their home for safety taking their two dogs Cooper and Maggie with them. They crawled into a protected corner just in time. After the tornado ripped through the farm they all emerged from the basement to nothing but menacing skies and bits of debris floating through the air above them. Their house and barns were gone along with the riding arena fence. Jumps were torn apart and strewn everywhere. Only one ancient shade tree, stripped of its leaves and some of its branches, remained standing in the front yard. Almost everything else on the farm was leveled. The family stood shaking and devastated, staring at the aftermath of the violent storm. It was then that they realized Lucy had disappeared.

Veronica felt panicked trying to find her mare. She walked the gently sloping hills around the pasture. Her parents joined her in the search. When it got dark they knew they had to stop for the night. It was too dangerous with all of the debris on the ground. They would have to try again the next day. It was a long night of waiting for Veronica and her parents staying at a neighbor's house since theirs was gone.

The next morning Veronica's father found Lucy alongside of the road a couple of miles from the farm. She was gone. Kevin drove the neighbor's pickup truck back to the house to tell Veronica hoping he could break the news gently. He knew his daughter would be hurting. He wanted to fix it for her but a dad can only do so much in a situation like that. He tearfully stood as strongly as he could as Veronica clung to him and cried. He hugged her for a long time. In a few minutes Sharon came into the room with tears running down her cheeks and joined the hug. All three were thankful that none of them was hurt even though they had lost Lucy.

Veronica had gotten Lucy a couple of years before and had dedicated herself to riding lessons from her instructor Tessa who came out to the farm every week. Now there was no Lucy and Veronica was grieving her awful death. She was distraught over how Lucy died, wondering how much she had suffered and been terrified during the minutes before she was killed. It broke her heart that her horse had to go through such a traumatic death.

It was several months before Veronica was able to get through the grieving process far enough to start over with another horse. She decided to focus on her school studies during the next semester and to wait and see how she would feel about getting a new horse. The next spring she felt like the time was right so she and Tessa searched for a different horse to love and train for competition on the show ring.

Grieving the Loss of Your horse from Old Age

Melissa's Story

I remember when my teenaged friend Melissa lost her wonderful, reliable horse Speckles. He was an older tall and lean flea-bitten gray gelding who had such a sweet disposition. He had lived a good long life on the quiet farm just down the road from the neighborhood we grew up in, and had given many children and teens a gentle start on their journeys to becoming accomplished riders. Melissa had ridden him on the trails close to the farm on many fun rides through the woods with me and the rest of the young horse owners at the farm.

Melissa was upset when she got a call from the farm owner that Speckles had died after she had gone home from the barn for the evening. She sobbed as she told me about losing him. He had been a faithful friend, one of those angel horses who take such good and kind-hearted care of their young riders.

Even though Melissa took the news hard that Speckles had died, she decided to get another horse right away. Her parents agreed and helped her purchase her new beautiful bay Thoroughbred horse Irish. She still missed Speckles and grieved for a long time but Irish became a good trusted friend too and she had him for many happy years.

It is Normal to Continue Grieving if You Get Another Horse

It is normal to continue grieving if you get another horse right away or if you wait a while before going through the process of choosing a new one. You may have a difficult time thinking about your new horse as a replacement for the older one who died. You may feel that no horse could ever replace her. And you are right. Your old horse was a unique creation of God and there will never be another one quite like her. And as a dedicated horse person, you have a big heart and more than likely there is room for more than one horse in your life although it may be a while before you are ready to find another one.

Your new horse will have his own personality quirks, fears, looks and the way he feels under saddle will be different. He will learn some training more quickly and some more slowly than your old horse. He will be good at some things your old horse could never seem to grasp. That may cause a twinge of pain in your heart because you might feel like it dishonors your memory of her. It is okay. You are not really dishonoring her memory. She would understand. And it is a normal part of the grieving process. In addition you will always have memories of how she excelled in her own talents.

Your new horse can still be a tremendous blessing while you grieve the loss of the old one. Each horse is with you for a season. Nothing can change that. Grieving is normal. Enjoying your new horse is normal and okay too.

Pre-Grieving the Loss of Your Horse

You may find yourself anticipating the death of an older or sick horse long before he actually dies and start the grieving process at that early point in time. That is normal too. If and when you get to that place remember to cherish what time you do have left with her. Take lots of pictures and videos. Save them in more than one place and more than one format so you will not lose those precious memories in case you might go through a fire, natural disaster or even lose boxes of pictures when you move to a new home. Save as many as you can using a cloud based storage system that will hold those precious memories even if your personal computer or cell phone quits working for good and you lose all of the information on them.

☐ Grieving the Loss of Your Horse Before and After Euthanasia

Amy and Jonathan's Story

Several years ago my friend Amy in Colorado faced the decision to have her son Jonathan's pony Charlie put down. The young boy had ridden Charlie almost every day through preschool and most of the way through kindergarten. But now the time had come when the elderly pony was going through insurmountable medical problems and keeping him alive left him in excruciating pain. Jonathan was at school when the veterinarian came out to the farm that day in the spring. Amy decided not to tell Jonathan about his pony's death until after he came home from school. He was so very angry and crying, stomping his feet and yelling, "Why?" to his mother over and over.

This was a heartbreaking day of decisions for Amy. She knew she had to have the pony put down and she had to decide when to tell Jonathan, before or after. That is a tough decision for any parent whose child has a beloved pony in bad condition. If you find yourself in this situation, you know your own child and what is best for him. If you are unsure of what and when to tell him, talk with other adults whom you trust who also know your child. And talk to other horse owners who have gone through the same heartache with their children. Make sure he is surrounded by supportive caring people. In many cases this may be the first time your child experiences death as well as the process of grieving after it happens and it can be an especially painful learning experience for him.

As Amy experienced, it is so difficult to make the decision to euthanize your horse or pony. Arm yourself with as much information as you can in the amount of time you have before the decision has to be made. Consult with your veterinarian about your horse's pain level, immediate and long term quality of life, the possibilities of treatment and other factors unique to your situation. Generally you will know in your heart and mind when it is time to euthanize him. It will be very painful to you but you will know when it is time to let him go and stop his suffering.

CHAPTER 4

ADVICE ABOUT ADVISING OTHER HORSE OWNERS FACED WITH THE EUTHANASIA DECISION

The following is a story about what to do and what not to do when a friend asks for your advice about whether or not to euthanize a horse.

Roberta's Story

My Texan friend Roberta had a hunter jumper farm near Waco where she taught riding to eager young students. She called me to ask my opinion when she was faced with the decision to euthanize one of her favorite school horses. One evening she found Buffy in excruciating colic pain, barely able to walk. Roberta put Buffy in the trailer and drove her to the veterinary clinic. Later, she called to ask me what I thought she should do. She told me about the possible treatment options that she and her veterinarian had discussed. We talked about Buffy's advanced age and other factors. Unfortunately, after weighing all of the information she told me, I gave Roberta my opinion and said it might be better to euthanize her. So Roberta took my advice and authorized her veterinarian to take that action.

Roberta immediately regretted her decision and felt that she should have first tried medical treatment for Buffy. She was such a good school horse that intensive medical treatment might have been the best choice. Euthanasia could have at least been postponed to give Buffy a chance to recover if it was possible.

Even though Roberta never vocally blamed me for my input into her decision, I felt awful about it. I never should have advised her to do it. So my advice about advising another horse owner about euthanasia is not to give your opinion as to whether it should be done. Instead, just listen to the outpouring of your friend's heart and empathize with her during the agonizing decision making process.

You can suggest that she consult her veterinarian to make sure she is clear about all of the treatment options and whether or not they are exhausted, but do not tell her whether to euthanize or not. Ask her if she has thought about getting a second opinion from another veterinarian. Give her a hug and a shoulder to cry on. Cry along with her. Tell her it is normal to be sad and angry about the situation. Carefully and patiently listen to how she feels about each option but do not lead her into any of them.

Stay patient and give her time and space as needed if she seems overwhelmed with talking about it. The decision has to be hers because she is the one who will have to live with it. If she takes complete ownership of the decision she will probably feel better about it in the long run no matter what she decides to do.

Sometimes a decision has to be made quickly if there has been a serious injury due to an accident or a sudden critical illness. And sometimes there is a window of a few hours or days, weeks or months before the decision has to be made. Be there for your friend as long as it takes before and after the outcome but absolutely do not make the decision for her.

CHAPTER 5

FACING THE EUTHANASIA DECISION WITH A TWEEN OR TEENAGED HORSE OWNER

If the horse owner at your farm is under the age of eighteen and facing this decision, make sure both of his parents are involved as much as possible. It is a good idea for the parents to discuss it between themselves and agree about the best way to be supportive. A teenager may or may not have the maturity to handle making this type of decision. He may protest loudly and angrily when the veterinarian advises euthanasia. He may try to hold in his feelings so others do not see them. Adults need to step in and surround him with love and care during this time. Unfortunately, his parents may have to force the decision on him if the situation is really bad.

It may seem like the right thing to do to tell your teen there will always be another horse but it will not help at that point. It will quite likely make his pain and grief worse to hear those words. He needs to live in that moment and get through the grieving process without having to think about a future horse until he feels he is ready. It hurts him too much to add that to the mix at that moment in time. He loves this horse and that is all that matters to him right now. Stay in the moment with him and comfort him.

You can talk about getting another horse later when the fresh, raw, intense pain has lessened. He may ask to buy a new horse in a couple of weeks. It may take a year. He may not want another horse at all for a long time. Be gentle when talking with him about it. Let him bring it up in conversation when he is ready to do so. Each child is as different as each adult is in the grieving process. He may not understand why he is experiencing such intense pain and anger. Tell him it is okay to take the time to grieve and that his feelings are normal for the experience he is going through.

Take extra care in monitoring her, maintaining an empathetic heart and being that soft place for her to fall during this already tumultuous teenaged season of life. Stay away from being a helicopter parent but at the same time remain available at any time to listen, hug and cry with her without judgment regarding her feelings about losing her horse or getting a new one.

CHAPTER 6

GRIEVING THE LOSS OF YOUR HORSE AFTER SELLING HIM

When I sold my horse Sunny I immediately regretted my decision. I still wish I had never sold him. I was eighteen years old at the time and sold him because my trainer Andrea pushed me to move on to a more challenging mount. I let the sale go through and immediately I was in a lot of emotional pain. I grieved Sunny for years wondering whatever happened to him. I replaced him right away borrowing my aunt's horse Tabby. She was a good horse but she could not replace Sunny. And after a few months I sent her back to my aunt's farm. It was too soon for me to think about getting another horse.

In my case, selling Sunny was the wrong choice, at the wrong time, for the wrong reason. There was a Sunny shaped hole in my heart and I never saw him again. And getting Tabby right away was also the wrong choice at the wrong time. If I could do it all over again I would not have given in to the pressure to sell him. I still occasionally go through all of the "what ifs", "could haves" and "should haves" of that decision in my mind. I felt like and still feel like I gave up my child for adoption. (*See note at the end of this chapter.) Ultimately it was my responsibility to make the choice to sell Sunny. My trainer pressured me, sure, but she did not hold a gun to my head!

Selling your horse is a personal choice. You have to weigh the pros and cons of selling or not and think through the consequences of either choice. Are you thinking about selling because you are in a financial bind? Are you selling because you want to change to a different caliber of horse for another level of horse show competition? Do you want to switch from one style of riding to another and feel that your current horse may not be the best choice for that challenge? Are you selling because of a major life change such as going to or graduating from college? Are you getting married or starting a family? Are you going through a divorce?   In some cases you may think that selling your horse is the best choice.   In other cases selling may not be necessary if your horse will fit into your plans and then you can avoid that grieving process.

If you choose to sell your horse, it may or may not cause you to grieve for a prolonged period of time.   It may be the perfect time to sell for you and you can move on seamlessly to your next horse with only momentary sadness.   You may bounce back fast.   Or you may feel pain you had not anticipated.   That is what happened to me.   If you have to sell, it can cause as much pain and grieving, sometimes even more than losing your horse to death.

If you decide to sell your horse you may go through regretting your decision and grieving just like I did.   You may have a lot of anger toward yourself for making such a crazy decision.   You may deeply regret selling your horse.   It may take a long time for you to get through the pain.

It has been long enough since I sold my horse that I know Sunny is no longer living on this earth.   It still makes me sad to think about it. Sometimes those feelings of sadness come back as if they are new and raw.   But I have gone on to ride many other good horses that I cared deeply about. And I look forward to seeing Sunny in Heaven. ☐

*I have always wondered how moms can get through the excruciating wounds of life after going through the painful process of giving up a child for adoption. It has to be infinitely worse than selling your horse.

CHAPTER 7

GRIEVING THE LOSS OF YOUR HORSE FROM COLIC

While colic itself is a symptom of and not a disease itself, it is too often implicated in the loss of a horse. Colic is a generalized term for pain in the abdomen of a horse somewhere on the continuum of mild to severe. Causes of colic include twisting or telescoping of the intestines, impaction of the digestive system, bloating from gas that cannot escape, etc. This can be induced by overfeeding or overwatering a hot and sweaty horse, changing food sources abruptly, ingesting sand if hay is fed on sandy ground, spoiled hay or grain, feeding too much grain in relation to hay and grass, prolonged use or accidental overdose of some types of medications, a high infestation of parasites, enteroliths (stones consisting of hydrous phosphates of magnesium, ammonia and iron), as well as unknown causes. In extremely rare circumstances an otherwise healthy horse can roll on the ground and initiate colic.

Colic can be so unpredictable. And while there are precautions you can take to help prevent colic, it can still happen. People can only control so many factors. Horses under expert care in the most ideal circumstances can still colic. Sometimes veterinary intervention can save them. Too often horses die.

Lynnette and Jackie's Story

Lynnette worked full time at a hunter-jumper farm in the southern part of Indiana. On an ordinary day she was bringing horses and ponies in from their pastures and dry lots for evening feeding. Little Daisy, a medium sized chestnut Welsh Pony was not in her normal spot at the gate where she usually stood anticipating her evening meal. When Lynnette went to get her she was standing off to the side breathing as if she was in a lot of pain. Lynnette noticed that she was sweating around her abdomen even though she had had a quiet day. She placed the halter on her head and tried to coax her to the gate. Little Daisy could barely move. She was clearly in a significant amount of pain. Lynnette managed to slowly get her into the barn and put her in crossties so she could call Jackie the farm owner. Then she quickly removed Little Daisy from the crossties and slowly walked her down the barn aisle to see if that would help ease the pain.

After answering Lynnette's call, Jackie stopped cooking dinner, turned off the stove, and ran outside the farmhouse across the yard through parking area to the barn. As soon as she saw the distressed pony she hooked up the two horse trailer to the pickup truck while simultaneously calling the veterinary school located ten miles away to let them know she was bringing a very sick pony as soon as she could get there.

Lynnette and Jackie carefully loaded Little Daisy into the trailer. Jackie headed the rig out of the driveway and on to the clinic. Lynnette stayed behind to finish bringing in the remaining horses and ponies to feed and water them. After making sure they were all okay and settled in for the night, Lynnette went home to take care of her own family.

At 9pm Jackie called Lynnette to tell her that Little Daisy was getting treatment but was still in bad condition. By 1am she still had not responded well. Jackie and the veterinarians on duty discussed options for further treatment. By 3am it was clear that they had done everything they could to try to save the sweet pony. Nothing was working. She was rapidly losing ground. Jackie decided at that point that Little Daisy would have to be put down rather than continue her suffering. The veterinarians at the school agreed that there was nothing else they could do for Little Daisy and that Jackie was making the right decision. It was heartbreaking and disappointing to all of them. They had lost the battle.

Jackie sadly took home Little Daisy's leather halter that had her brass nameplate on it along with the empty trailer. The whole experience stabbed her in the heart. She decided to wait until Lynnette came to work in the morning to tell her what happened. In the meantime she cried herself to sleep.

Jackie had lost other horses and ponies before. A couple of them had also colicked. It never got any easier. Each horse and pony was special to her. Little Daisy was special too. Jackie had given many riding lessons to children who rode Little Daisy. It was always such a delight to see each child jump a fence for the first time riding the always reliable pony. The sweet pony had been a patient teacher. She was always cooperative and never got grumpy with anyone. Tears flooded Jackie's eyes as she thought about all of the children who had ridden Little Daisy. Most of them had grown too big for her and had moved on to riding larger ponies and horses. She knew that all of them would be sad to hear that Little Daisy was gone.

The next morning Lynnette arrived early at the farm and walked up to the house knowing Jackie would already be up working in her home office. She walked right in because Jackie had an open door policy and a welcoming heart. Lynnette knew as soon as she saw her face that the news about Little Daisy was bad. They both teared up as Jackie explained what happened.

Then Jackie went back to work on her computer and Lynnette went out to the barn to start feeding and turning out horses and ponies. A sorrow filled lump formed in her throat every time she walked past Little Daisy's empty stall.

Clyde, the resident black lab could tell something was amiss and stayed close by Lynnette's side as she worked distributing grain and hay, filled water buckets and troughs and mucked out stalls. Lynnette always appreciated Clyde's company and felt comforted by him today. He had a heart of gold. She gave him extra hugs and treats to thank him.

When the children, turned loose from school for the day, came to the farm for riding lessons with their parents that afternoon, Jackie and Lynnette gently explained that Little Daisy had gotten terribly sick and died. All of them were sad. Some cried. And some asked questions that Jackie and Lynnette answered the best they could. They told the kids that she was not suffering anymore and that she was happy and in Heaven.

Most of the children went on with their riding lessons, some of them learning to ride different ponies who replaced Little Daisy. It was an emotional adjustment for each of them in varying ways. They all went on to fondly remember Little Daisy.

Brittany's Story

Brittany had a 6 year old gelding named Jet. He was beautiful and a lot of people smiled and said so when they saw him. He was jet black with four white stockings and a symmetrical star on his forehead that was perfectly placed and just the right size. He was well-behaved and eager to do whatever Brittany asked of him. His conformation was as close to perfect as you could get. He was a joy to ride. To everyone's surprise he won both halter and performance classes.

Jet was the perfect horse in every way except one. He had a history of colicking multiple times over the past couple of years. Brittany took excellent care of him. She followed her veterinarian's recommendations to the letter regarding what to feed him, at what times and how much at a time. She always made sure he was completely cooled down after a ride and kept a sharp eye on him in the process. She slowly introduced him to anything new to eat. She made sure he had good water and carefully doled it out in small portions when he was hot. The soil in her fields was not sandy. She had it tested for composition and the results were about as good as you would want. Jet did not chew wood or crib. Brittany's dry lots had no sand or gravel in them. Jet's colic was a mystery.

Midmorning on a beautiful summer day, Brittany worked on barn chores, satisfied with crossing tasks off of her to-do list as she finished each one. One of her saddles needed some extra attention so she sat down on a stool in the tack room after grabbing her leather care supplies and began to clean it. The barn was quiet. She could hear her horses munching on an early snack of timothy and clover mixed hay that Brittany had carefully inspected beforehand. She could hear water running intermittently as the automated system refilled the bowls in the stalls. She reached down to pet Bootsy, her affectionate barn cat, who rubbed against her leg. The chores were almost done and she looked forward to a short ride on Jet before lunch. It was a great day, she smiled to herself.

The amplified ring of the landline in the barn jolted Brittany to her feet. It was Casey, her farrier. They talked about when would be the best time for him to come out to shoe her horses later in the week. They also talked for several minutes about an upcoming regional horse show they both planned to attend, razzing each other about who would make or lose the most money at the event. Brittany planned to show Jet. Casey planned to shoe horses as well as spend the money for his son Carson to show his horse Red. The teen and his horse were a surprisingly good team. Brittany and Carson showed in different classes so they both had a chance to beat their respective competition.

Brittany hung up the phone and walked back over to finish cleaning her saddle. A few minutes later she noticed noise contrasting with the previous quiet of the barn. One of the horses was kicking the wall. She ran down the barn aisle to find that Jet was the one kicking. He was also sweating and in pain from colic. Again! Alarmed, Brittany called her veterinarian. Dr. Peterson's office was only two miles away so he came right over.

Dr. Peterson found Brittany walking Jet in the shade of the trees in front of the barn. Her eyes betrayed the anxiety she was experiencing. He talked with Brittany as he carefully examined Jet. Brittany appreciated his thoroughness and care for Jet. Dr. Peterson had a calm and gentle spirit.

"He seemed fine an hour ago," Brittany offered. "I called you as soon as I noticed he was hurting." She felt guilty even though she was doing everything Dr. Peterson had advised to keep Jet from colicking. She still felt like she was a bad horse mom. She hoped there was something the veterinarian and she could do to fix this continuing problem.

Dr. Peterson must have been reading her mind. "Brittany, I don't know of anyone who takes better care of their horses. This is not your fault. Jet's colic is a conundrum. I think it is time to take him to the clinic to run some tests to see if we can get to the root cause of this. What are your thoughts?" His kind eyes gave her a comforting look through the top of his bifocals.

"Yes, I agree. This has happened too many times. I want to know more of what is going on. And he seems to be in more pain than I have seen him in before." Brittany brushed her hair out of her face and then rubbed Jet's neck.

"I will give him a painkiller now. Then we can transport him to the clinic. Is your two horse trailer ready to go? If not, I can call Tracey at the office. She can bring ours over if you would like." He gave Jet the syringe of painkiller. Jet did not even flinch at the poke if the needle.

"I cleaned it out and checked it this morning while I was working on barn chores. It was the first thing I crossed off of my to-do list. If you don't mind holding Jet, I will hook it up to the truck and be ready to load in a couple of minutes." Brittany handed the lead rope to Dr. Peterson and started jogging over to the truck before she finished her last sentence. She felt relieved to have Dr. Peterson to take care of Jet and that his state of the art clinic was so close by.

They loaded Jet carefully into the trailer. Brittany followed Dr. Peterson to the Town and Country Veterinary Clinic. When they got there Jet was feeling some relief from the pain. It was easier for him to walk when they unloaded him. They took him to a clean comfortable, climate controlled stall outfitted with cameras for observation. Brittany stroked his neck and kissed his velvety nose. Then she left him with Dr. Peterson and walked down the hallway through the double doors to the front desk to fill out Jet's paperwork. She could see him on one of the monitors above the counter. That gave her further reassurance that he would be watched in case he needed hands on attention in a hurry.

A few minutes later Brittany went back to Jet's stall, making sure he was okay. Dr. Peterson, joined by his vet tech Josh, went over the tests they would run including radiographs and ultrasound along with blood work, etc. Brittany listened intently to each word, confident that Dr. Peterson could fix whatever was causing Jet to be in so much pain.

When they finished talking about the tests Brittany had to go home to take care of the other horses and her cat. She gave her horse a light and gentle hug and said," I'll be back to get you soon, Jet Man." She started to walk back to the truck, hesitated, and gave Jet another pat on the nose. Leaving him behind increased her anxiety. She trusted Dr. Peterson and his staff but at the same time she felt the weight of worrying about poor Jet.

Back at home Brittany fed her other horses and her cat Bootsy. She turned out the horses for the night when they finished their grain. The weather was supposed to be calm and cool. She picked out the stalls and sprinkled lime on the manure pile to help combat flies. She wiped out the water bowls in the stalls. The horses settled down to graze in the waning sunlight. Everything at the farm was peaceful except for Brittany's thoughts.

She walked back to the house and tackled her messy kitchen. Anxiety about Jet drove her to keep busy so she tried to do some work on her computer but she could not concentrate. Her thoughts were consumed with Jet and what he was going through. So she switched back to house work, vacuuming the floors and the spider webs all around the crown molding that reappear all too quickly even with the best pest control. Then she cleaned her bathroom, sorting through makeup and hair products, tossing out of date items and reorganizing what was left. She had gotten some helpful tips on how to do this from Kay Patterson on the YouTube channel "The Organized Soprano." Kay, also a horse person, seemed like a good friend even though they had never met. (*See note at the end of this chapter.) And cleaning and organizing had always been Brittany's "go to" when she felt stressed out. It usually helped calm her racing mind in good times and bad.

Brittany moved to the living room with her cleaning supplies and straightened out the pillows on the couch giving each one a stress relieving karate chop. Just as she cleared some left over breakfast dishes from the coffee table the phone rang. Her heart skipped a beat. She picked up the phone from the side table to hear Dr. Peterson's voice on the other end. After briefly exchanging pleasantries he explained what was going on with Jet at that point in time.

"Brittany, we did radiographs and an ultrasound. There is something in Jet's abdomen the size of a softball that is blocking his colon. Dr. Delph also looked at the scans. She and I both agree that surgery to remove it would be the next best step. That is most likely what is causing Jet to colic."

"Is it some kind of cancer?" Brittany asked, her brow wrinkling with concern.

Dr. Peterson said, "We do not think so. Given where it is located, in the small colon, it may be an enterolith – a stone that has formed over time. They can cause episodic colic symptoms like Jet has experienced over the past couple of years."

Brittany felt a little relieved that it was unlikely to be cancer but an enterolith sounded bad too, along with the risk of surgery. "When can you do surgery on him? Tomorrow?"

"As soon as possible tonight is best. Since his symptoms are worse this time we do not want to wait."

"Of course! What should I do? Should I come over there?" Brittany wanted to do something to help poor Jet.

"Since you are only two miles away we can call you with updates. And you can get here quickly if need be. There is really not any reason for you to have to come over right now."

Brittany reluctantly agreed. There was nothing to do in the clinic waiting room but worry. Knowing that she would not be able to sleep that night she continued to clean her house. She collapsed on the couch in time to watch the 10pm news but she was not listening. She could not focus on anything but Jet.

At quarter after ten the phone rang and she jumped to her feet. It was Dr. Delph who had left Dr. Peterson in surgery with Jet. She said they had removed the enterolith and were working on removing some damaged tissue. It was more complicated than they first thought. They would call again as soon as they knew more.

Brittany's anxiety ramped up again. Damaged tissue, she thought to herself. That sounded scary. She could not stay at home any longer. It was too hard. So she packed a drink, some snacks and a book to try to read while she sat in the waiting room. She called the clinic to tell them she was coming but only got their voicemail. She left a message instead, not sure if they would check it before she got there. She went out to the truck and unhitched the trailer knowing she would not be bringing Jet home for at least a few days. She hopped in the driver's seat and headed to the clinic.

Five minutes later Josh the vet tech let her in the front door. He had listened to her message and waited for her. She walked in and he locked the door behind her. Josh did not know anything more to tell Brittany. He left her in the waiting room and went back through the double doors to the surgical suite.

The waiting room was starkly quiet. Brittany could hear her heart pounding. She didn't open her book. She paced the floor instead, stopping at each of the veterinary posters on the walls. She stared through them instead of comprehending what they said. She could only think about Jet. She prayed that he would be okay.

Twenty minutes later Dr. Peterson walked through the back door of the waiting room. Brittany got a lump in her throat as she saw the look on his face. This could not be good. Her heart sank.

"I am so sorry, Brittany," the veterinarian gently said, "There was so much damaged tissue that Dr. Delph and I could not save him. He lost too much blood. There was nothing else we could do."

"No!" Brittany exclaimed, her eyes welling up with tears. "We took good care of him. I did everything you told me to do. You did everything you knew to do. This couldn't be!"

"There is no good explanation for it, Brittany," Dr. Peterson said softly. "We all did what we could, the best we knew how." He felt that his words were inadequate at best. He felt so badly for Brittany.

"I bought Jet as a four year old. Maybe the stone started before that."

"Yes, that sounds very likely. Enteroliths can start in foals. It may have been there that early." Changing the subject Dr. Peterson went on," Is there anything we can do for you, Brittany. This is a rough thing to go through. We would like to help in any way that we can."

Brittany appreciated his kindness. "I am trying to figure out what to do now." She hesitated while Dr. Peterson waited and listened. "Can Jet be cremated? Then maybe I can bury him on the farm." It hurt her so much to voice those words but she wanted so badly for Jet to come home where he had been happy and loved.

"Yes, we can take care of that for you," he gently replied. Dr. Peterson felt it was important to make the arrangements for Brittany and others who had lost animals he had helped care for. He knew it could help get her through the grieving process. He had seen too many people go through losing their horses and other beloved animals. It still broke his heart every time he lost one in his practice. It was the one part of his work he dreaded.

Brittany drove home. The short drive seemed to take a long time. She was numb and simply going through the motions of navigation. The radio was silent. She could not stand listening to any music or chatty talk shows under the circumstances. She felt disconnected from the rest of the world in her grief. Losing Jet syphoned the joy out of her life. When she got home she felt like her whole body had turned into a useless pile of rocks. She dragged herself into the house and took a shower until the hot water ran out. As soon as she climbed into bed the dam in her brain holding back the tears broke. Her sweet, beautiful Jet was gone! Jet was gone and there was nothing she or anyone else could do about it. Brittany cried herself to sleep.

The next morning Brittany woke up about an hour later than usual. She had been dreaming and it took her a few moments to get her bearings. Then it hit her hard again that Jet was gone. She pushed herself to get up to take care of the other horses and her cat. If it had not been for them she would have stayed in bed. Since the horses were still out grazing in the pasture from the night before, coming in for grain an hour later than usual did not cause any problems for them although Bootsy was a bit fussy about not getting fed on time. Brittany quickly poured out food into her bowl and she began nibbling.

Brittany set up hay and grain in each stall double checking water bowls as she went down the barn aisle. She felt a pang in her heart as she glanced into Jet's empty stall and caught herself as she almost automatically put grain in his bucket. Then she realized she had already set up his hay. She gulped back a sob. After bringing in the horses she went back to the house and collapsed into her favorite chair allowing herself to cry once again.

Several days later Tracey called from the vet clinic. Jet had been cremated and his ashes were ready for Brittany to take home. With a broken heart she drove to the clinic. She had picked out a beautiful wooden box style urn online the day after Jet died. His name was inscribed surrounded by a chiseled silhouette of his head taken from a painting by one of Brittany's friends. It was a fitting memorial for Jet. There would never be another horse like him.

Brittany took Jet home and could not decide what to do with his ashes. Should she find a place in the house for his urn? Would she bury him? She had thought about it since the night he died but it was too soon and too overwhelming to make that choice. Temporarily she put the box on the credenza in her home office and postponed making a permanent decision until an undetermined point in the future.

It took a long time for Brittany to get through the shock of losing Jet so suddenly. She went to the horse show that she had talked about with her farrier Casey. She felt empty because Jet was not there. Casey's son Carson showed his horse Red and they won their division. Brittany went through the motions of cheering them on and congratulating them at the end of the show. She did not want her emptiness to dampen the celebration of anyone else's success.

Eventually Brittany regained her desire to find another horse to show and love. She took home a beautiful three year old mare named Rosemary and began to earn her trust and train her. She fit right in with the other horses. And Rosemary helped to heal Brittany's broken heart.

Losing a horse to any cause of colic is tragic and so unpredictable. There is no way to prepare yourself for it other than to know that it happens to some horses. Even horses that have expert care may die from it. We can only hope that cures are found for the many causes and do the best we can to get through the grieving process if it does happen to any of our own horses.

* Kay Patterson is a real person who also has a history with loving horses and her Youtube channel "The Organized Soprano" is the author's favorite.

CHAPTER 8

GRIEVING THE LOSS OF YOUR HORSE FROM LAMINITIS AND HOOF ABSCESSES

Laminitis (Founder) can be a chronic problem for horses once it starts. Hoof abscesses, infection built up from bacteria entering the hoof, can also be a chronic problem in some cases, resulting from laminitis and may also be a result of poor hoof care or other causes. Laminitis can be caused by nutritional imbalances, sudden access to large amounts of spring grass or grain, a new diet, an illness, retained placenta in mares, too much riding on hard surfaces, a major episode of colic, foot injuries and diseases, the use of black walnut bedding, etc. And sometimes the cause cannot be determined.

Your veterinarian and farrier can examine your horse for signs of Acute Laminitis, Chronic Laminitis and hoof abscesses. They can treat your horse and advise you on care and feeding options to alleviate and prevent problems in the future.

Matt's Story

Matt owned a mare named Speedy Dream who was pretty good at barrel racing. She was fast at a flat out run and agile around the barrels. She won a lot of ribbons and trophies in competition. She stayed calm and focused when Matt trained her at home. In the show ring she remained unflappable in the midst of screaming spectators. She followed him around the farm like a puppy as Matt checked fences, filled water troughs and fed the horses and various other animals on the farm where he boarded his horse. The chores helped Matt pay Speedy Dream's bills and he could spend more time with her in the process, giving them both a break from training and competitions. They both enjoyed their quality time together.

Matt was getting Speedy Dream tuned up for an upcoming horse show when he noticed that she was a little off of her game as he walked and jogged her to warm her up a few days before the show. He could feel her limping just slightly and watched her head bob a little crookedly from his position in the saddle. He dismounted, took her back into the barn and tied her next to her stall. He carefully removed her saddle, bridle and boots. Then he moved her to the wash racks and slowly hosed her down. He looked her over and felt for heat in her legs and feet. He could not find anything alarming, just that slight limp. He asked his friend Julie to take a look as he jogged Speedy Dream from the ground but she only saw the slight limp. Neither one of them thought it was anything serious.

Matt kept an eye on Speedy Dream. The limping did not seem to get any better or worse over the next few days. He decided not to take her to the horse show and let her rest from training for a little while. Her stall opened into a one acre paddock so she could come and go as she pleased. It was separated from the main pastures where groups of horses were turned out together. It was a good place to graze and relax for Speedy Dream.

Even though Matt decided not to take Speedy Dream to the horse show he still wanted to go. Some of the other boarders were taking their horses so he hitched a ride with one of them, leaving Speedy Dream to her own devices. Matt enjoyed helping his friends with their horses at shows. Things could get pretty crazy while everyone was scrambling to get dressed, groom and tack up as well as be at the right place at the right time, not to mention making sure both horses and humans were fed and got enough water to drink at the appropriate times. Matt appreciated all of the help he got at shows so he wanted to pitch in where he could since his mare was not going.

Matt hauled buckets of water for horses and refilled water bottles for riders. He checked girths and bridles and walked horses while riders grabbed snacks at the concession stand. At the end of the day he helped pack equipment and load horses into the farm's large trailer for the hour long drive home.

When they got back to the farm Julie's horse Marble was the first one out of the trailer. She grabbed his lead rope and led him into the barn. She flipped on the light switch and gasped. The barn aisle was a mess. It had been clean when they left for the show that morning. It was a disaster area. There was hay and bedding all over. Grooming kits were apart and strewn everywhere. Several stall doors were unlatched. Some were wide open including Speedy Dream's. Matt and she had double checked to make sure all doors were latched the last thing before they went to the show. What on Earth had happened?

Julie yelled for Matt who was helping unload the other horses. He quickly walked into the barn to find Julie closing and latching Speedy Dream's stall door.

"I don't know where she is," exclaimed Julie. "Maybe she is in her paddock."

Matt turned on the floodlights and walked outside through the back door of her stall to her paddock. Speedy Dream was not there. At that point he was not too alarmed. She had to be somewhere. He walked back into the barn aisle and wondered aloud why it was such a mess.

"Julie, she is not in her paddock. What is going on with this place?" he asked as he stopped by Marble's stall for a second where Julie unwrapped his legs to get him ready to turn out in the field.

"It looks like someone had a party. I'll help you find her." Julie grabbed all of Marble's leg wraps and dumped them by the washing machine in the tack room and put her horse in his stall before joining Matt in the search.

The skies were clear so none of the other horses who had stayed home from the show had been in their stalls when they left. All of them had been turned out in the pastures for the day. Speedy Dream was the only one missing. Julie and Matt checked the stalls, closed and latched the doors as they went down the aisle searching for the missing mare. Meanwhile each of the other boarders brought their horses in, all astonished at the disarray.

When Matt and Julie got to the end of the aisle they found the door to the feed room open. And it was a mess too. There were torn bags of sweet feed and corn. Bales of hay were broken open and tumbled from the stack. Supplement tubs were dumped over. It looked nothing like the clean and organized room that Matt had left that morning when he finished feeding everyone.

After some more searching, Julie and Matt found Speedy Dream lying down, moaning in pain, in the riding ring. The gate to the ring had also been left open by someone, but whom?

Matt called their veterinarian to take care of his mare while Julie marched up to the farm house to talk to Al who owned the farm to see if he knew what had happened. She walked in without bothering to knock and found him washing dishes in the kitchen.

Julie explained to Al the condition of the barn. "I don't get this." She was perplexed. "What happened here while we were all gone to the show today?"

Al sighed and responded, "The grandkids are here today. I thought they were just playing. I didn't know they were wrecking the barn."

"They wrecked more than just the barn, Al. Matt's horse apparently got into the feed room and ate until she got sick. Her stall door was open as well as the feed room door. When we left this morning everything was in apple pie order. You know we are all so careful about doors and gates. Why did you let the kids play out there without supervision?"

Al grimaced, grabbed a towel and dried his hands. Then he walked over to the stairway up to the bonus room where the kids were playing video games. "Laney! Ethan! Travis! Get down here!" he yelled.

All three of the kids thundered down the steps wide-eyed, knowing they were in trouble. They were not sure for what because they knew they had probably broken several rules and did not know which one raised an alarm for Granddaddy Al.

"Were you playing in the barn today?" Al asked gruffly.

"Ethan and Travis were," Laney piped up.

"You were too!" Both boys glared at her.

"Okay, now that we have established that all three of you were playing in the barn, did you open the stall doors and the door to the feed room?"

All three shrugged their shoulders in response. The wide eyes continued on their faces.

"I need some answers because one of the horses got out of her stall and went into the feed room and ate too much grain and now she is very sick. The veterinarian is going to have to take care of her."

"That's impossible, Granddaddy! All of the horses went to the show today!" Travis exclaimed.

"No, Travis, not all of them went," Julie firmly stated.

"Speedy Dream stayed home because she was limping and Matt didn't take her."

"Well, she wasn't in her stall when we were playing in the barn," said Ethan.

"That is because the back door to her paddock was open so she could go in and out of her stall," Julie explained in exasperation.

Al was furious. "You kids are not supposed to play in the barn at all! All three of you are going to pay for the veterinary bills even if you have to muck stalls for a year!

"Right now you need to go out to the barn and find Matt and apologize for you irresponsible behavior. And I will go with you to make sure you do that. Then I am going to call your parents to tell them what happened."

Al stomped out of the house quickly followed by the three wide eyed kids who were dreading all of the consequences ahead of them. Julie went with them to make sure Al backed up his words with decisive actions.

A few minutes later the five of them found Matt with Speedy Dream. He had tears in his eyes. His mare was obviously in pain, stretching out her front feet and shifting her weight to her haunches. Matt was slowly coaxing her into the barn.

Al sternly told the kids to apologize. Laney and Ethan both burst into tears. All three said they were sorry. Then Al made them clean up the mess. They moaned and groaned and began the enormous job ahead of them.

Al looked at the poor mare and saw a fresh gash on one of her legs. She had gotten cut by something during her disastrous day alone. He was angry. "I am so sorry the kids did this to your horse, Matt. This is my fault for not watching them closer. Have you called Dr. Hilliard yet?"

"Yes, Al, as soon as we found her lying in the riding ring." Matt was angry too but his focus was on helping Speedy Dream so he kept his thoughts to himself about the children and what they had done.

"I am going to make sure those kids pay for this. I am going to talk with their parents about consequences."

"Thank you, Al. I appreciate you taking care of it. I hope Speedy Dream will recover quickly so the bills are not too terrible."

"Me too, Matt. This is more than just an inconvenience. Speedy Dream is part of your family, our family here at the farm. None of us wants her to suffer needlessly."

Their conversation was interrupted by the sound of Dr. Hilliard's van outside the barn. Al walked out to greet him and explain briefly what happened and urged the veterinarian to send all of the bills to him for Speedy Dream's care. The veterinarian agreed to send copies to both Matt and him. He wrote it in his notes for the mare.

They walked into the barn to find her on the ground again with Matt kneeling next to her stroking her neck. Dr. Hilliard examined her finding heat in all four feet with strong pulses at her sesamoids. He asked for more details about what had happened and came to the conclusion that she had gotten into the feed room early in the day and now had acute laminitis from eating a large amount of sweet feed.

"She will need a lot of care, special nutrition and monitoring over the next few weeks to help her through this. She is a pretty sick horse. After I get her started on medications and other treatment I will leave her in your care until the morning. You can call me anytime and I'll come back out. I am available all night. I will work on the laceration on her leg before I leave, too. It looks like it will be okay and not need any stitches.

"By the way, who is your farrier?"

"George Stern," Matt replied.

"George has a good reputation. I will give him a call so we can coordinate treatment for your horse." Dr. Hilliard knew George was quite knowledgeable and had a lot of experience working with serious hoof problems.

Dr. Hilliard finished treating Speedy Dream for the night. She felt better after some pain medication and stood up on her own. They moved her into a larger stall usually set up for broodmares ready to foal. It had a webcam set up that would help with monitoring the mare's condition. Dr. Hilliard, Matt and Al could all watch her from their phones or computers.

Even with the app on his phone, Matt decided to stay the night. He asked Julie to stay with Speedy Dream while he went home to shower, get some food and pack a bag. While Julie waited for him to come back she downloaded the app to her phone so she could help watch the mare.

Al walked back to the farm house and called his son Jason and daughter in law Sarah to tell them what the kids had done. They were understandably appalled and agreed to pay for the vet bills, lost grain hay and supplements and other damages to the barn. They also assured Al that the children would participate in earning the money to pay the bills as well as lose privileges. And they would no longer be allowed to visit Granddaddy Al's farm without direct parental supervision.

Jason and Sarah drove to the farm and picked up the kids and explained to them what trouble they had caused and what the consequences would be. They wanted them to know that Mom and Dad were on the same page and no whining or protesting would be tolerated.

Laney, Ethan and Travis were upset because Speedy Dream was so sick. Laney and Ethan started crying again. Travis fiercely blinked back tears. All three also realized the fun they had been having had come to a screeching halt. The next few weeks and months would not be fun at all. Extra chores! No cell phones! No video games! Grounded from playing with friends!

Life was going to be hard and boring for as far as they could see into the future. It looked like forever in their young minds.

Meanwhile Matt came back to the farm for the night. He walked in to find Julie softly brushing Speedy Dream's back. Before she left she told Matt she would be back in the morning so he could go home and get some rest. Matt appreciated his friend pitching in to take care of his mare.

Julie went home and took a shower while her thoughts went from concern about Speedy Dream to anger and frustration regarding the kids and Al. There was no excuse, she thought. It should not have happened. A few minutes later she fell into bed, too tired from all of the day's events to fight sleeping.

Matt did not get much sleep while keeping an eye on Speedy Dream. She spent most of the night lying down in the deep poplar bedding. He checked her feet frequently to see how hot they were. He followed Dr. Hilliard's instructions on what he needed to do to help her. In between he dozed off in a lawn chair outside her of stall.

In the morning Julie checked the webcam app on her phone. She saw Speedy Dream lying down, momentarily breathing hard. She sighed at the needless pain the mare must be feeling. She quickly dressed, then drove her small blue sedan to Franny's Fast Food to get some breakfast sandwiches, a large orange juice for Matt and an espresso for herself. Then she headed through the winding suburban streets that opened up into the neighboring rural area where the boarding farm was located. She pulled into the farm lane and frowned as she passed Al's house, her anger and frustration unabated.

When Matt heard the familiar hum of the blue sedan's engine he got up from the lawn chair and met Julie at the big door at the end of the barn. As they sat on a tack trunk eating breakfast he filled her in on Speedy Dream's condition and treatment since Julie had left the night before. As they finished the food they heard another vehicle stop outside the barn. Dr. Hilliard walked in a minute later. Matt simultaneously felt relieved and anxious upon seeing him – relieved because the veterinarian was there to help and anxious because of the reality that Speedy Dream was so sick that she needed his expert care.

After Dr. Hilliard checked the mare he gave Matt more instructions on feeding, administering medications and other care for his horse. Matt wrote everything down in the notebook he was using to track Speedy Dream's progress including medications diet and water intake. It was the same notebook he had used to track her training progress and performance at horse shows. He thought to himself that it was a sad reminder of what used to be.

Dr. Hilliard interrupted Matt's thoughts, "I talked with George Stern last night. He can come out first thing tomorrow to look at Speedy Dream's feet. I brought my X-ray machine to get some pictures so we can plan what to do together."

"That sounds good. I will be here tomorrow," Matt responded, glad that the expert farrier was also going to help his horse.

"I can be here too," Julie added. She and Matt had already worked out a schedule for the next couple of weeks so Speedy Dream would not be alone while she was so sick.

Dr. Hilliard got his X-ray machine out of his van while Matt and Julie carefully convinced the hurting mare to stand long enough to take pictures of the bones in her feet. After taking the pictures Dr. Hilliard went home to get ready for church.

Before Matt left he fed and watered all of the horses, and picked out their stalls while Julie fed and watered the other farm animals. It was a long day for Julie but other boarders who were in and out all day broke the monotony. And she had her own online business to keep her occupied on her notebook computer. That would work out fine for as long as Speedy Dream needed constant monitoring and medications. Matt slept during the day and came back in time to feed in the evenings, stayed all night and went home after feeding in the morning. This went on for the first couple of weeks until the mare was out of immediate danger of any other complications.

Since Speedy Dream did not seem to need as much attention, Matt and Julie both went back to their normal routines. Dr. Hilliard decided to only examine the mare once a week unless something came up. George had been out to work on her feet a couple of times and decided to give her a couple of weeks before he checked her again. Her condition seemed to stabilize without much change for the next month. She was on her feet a little more each day. Matt was more confident that he would someday ride her again.

It seemed like things were getting better but suddenly things got worse. Speedy Dream laid down more and showed increased pain in her feet, especially when using hoof testers. It started in the foot that the mare had been favoring when she started limping before she had acute laminitis. Pain in the other feet quickly followed the next day. She was in excruciating pain.

Matt called Dr. Hilliard. He came out quickly to assess the situation. Julie was already there. She had just given Marble a bath and was hand grazing him while he dried off when the veterinarian arrived. She clucked to Marble and gently steered him into his stall and walked over to stand next to Matt to see what was going on.

Dr. Hilliard gave Speedy Dream some medication in the middle of examining her because her pain response was so strong. He stopped and waited for her to relax as the medication took effect. But it barely took the edge off of her pain. He continued to examine her to determine what to do next. He retrieved his x-ray equipment from the van and took radiographs of her feet. He looked carefully at the screen with concern about the changes he saw. He looked at the mare again. Then he called George and talked with him a few minutes as Matt and Julie stood next to the mare.

He put his phone back in his pocket and grabbed the x-ray equipment. "I am going to put this back in the van. I will be back in a minute." He wanted to collect his thoughts before he said anything else.

Matt and Julie gave each other worried looks. Speedy Dream laid down again with a groan and snorted, wiggling her legs and head trying to get comfortable without success. She gave up and laid down breathing hard.

Dr. Hilliard walked back into the barn and approaching Matt and Julie, he said, "I am very concerned about Speedy Dream's condition. The radiographs show that even with all of the treatment she has had including George's expert care, her feet are severely damaged. And even though she was on antibiotics as well as other medications she now has severe abscesses. The infection has taken over her feet."

Matt asked, "What does this mean? Do I need to retire her and not ride her again?"

The veterinarian replied, "Her feet are in such bad condition and she is in so much pain. We do not have any stronger pain medication to use. What I gave her an hour ago has not helped her." The concern in his eyes emphasized his gently spoken words.

With tear filled eyes Matt asked a question he dreaded. "Do we need to put her down?"

"That is probably the best thing to do for her," Dr. Hilliard responded. "We are out of other options at this point. I wish I had a better answer for you." He hesitated, giving Matt time to think.

Matt looked at Julie. She had tears in her eyes too. This is so hard, Matt thought to himself. It was devastating! After hesitating for several minutes he agreed to let Speedy Dream go. As painful as it was for him he could not stand the thought of her suffering anymore with no hope for a better future.

Julie said, "I'll go talk to Al." She and Matt both knew that he had his own back hoe and could take care of burying Speedy Dream on the farm.

Matt winced and said in a whisper, "Yes, please Julie. I don't think I can talk to him…..This just doesn't seem real." He turned his attention to the mare he loved so much as tears started streaming down his face. He gently caressed her.

Julie walked out of the barn and over to the farmhouse. She knocked on the door then entered the front hall without waiting. "Al! Speedy Dream is in really bad shape! Dr. Hilliard is going to put her down."

Al appeared from the kitchen and listened to what Julie had to say. "I'll take care of her burial," he said as he started to pull on his boots. His heart was heavy with the weight of what was happening. I feel so sorry for poor Speedy Dream and Matt, he thought to himself.

"You need to figure out what to do about the kids too since their actions caused this situation. I feel sorry for them. This is a terrible thing to happen for them as well as Matt."

"I do not know what to tell them, Julie. I will call their parents later to see what they have to say about the situation," Al offered softly. "They are just kids."

"That would be the best thing to do. I am going back out so I can be there for Matt. This is tearing him apart." Julie left the house.

After it was over Matt and Julie hugged each other and cried. They both knew there was never going to be another Speedy Dream. She was one of a kind. It left a big horse shaped hole in Matt's heart.

Later that evening Al called Jason and Sarah to tell them what had happened. The three of them decided not to tell the children that Speedy Dream had died unless and until they asked. They were so young to have to go through such a hard life lesson.

And they agreed that if any of the three asked they would tell all of them what happened to avoid one child being burdened with secrecy and possibly sharing the information without the others being prepared by caring parents.

When he finished the conversation with Jason and Sarah, Al called Matt and apologized again for everything that happened. He told Matt he would buy him another horse of his choice when he was ready to get one again. He also told him about how they were going to approach the situation with Laney, Ethan and Travis. Matt felt compassion for them and agreed with how the adults were going to handle it.

Matt continued working at the farm even though Speedy Dream was gone. He was not ready to get another horse of his own for a long time but he still wanted to continue taking care of the other horses and animals. Julie and his other friends still had their horses at the farm. And he wanted to go to more horse shows with them. He saved the extra money he earned and put it in his "Someday Fund" for when he was ready to get another horse in the future.

Cassie and Chad's Story

Cassie was playing solitaire on her cell phone when it rang just as she was about to break her record score. But the interruption was good. It was DJ at the horse rescue farm Saving Angels Horse Sanctuary.

"Cassie! We rescued the mare from the kill pen that you wanted!" DJ was half out of breath from excitement, so happy to save another horse.

"Oh, thank you!" Cassie had been waiting on pins and needles hoping against hope that the mare could be saved. She had seen a picture of her on a popular horse rescue web site and the horse had tugged at her heart strings. She had to save her!

The mare had been at a kill pen where DJ and Her husband Hans rescued horses on a regular basis in the southwestern part of the US. The mare for Cassie was one of eight they had brought home this time. Now they were all safe at the Sanctuary, each waiting for a new home.

Cassie had a stall ready for the new mare. She and her husband Chad had a six stall barn on their fifteen acre farm in northwestern Georgia where they also lived in an old remodeled

1930s house built from a kit. They already had four other horses, Rocky, Caleb, Phoebe and Rueben, and a pony named Owen. And to protect them from predators in the area they had two Great Pyrenees dogs Mack and Pete. They also had a goat named Otis who liked to hang out with the horses.

Chad and Cassie had built the barn themselves. Both of them had horses when they were children and neither ever got over the addiction. From the time that the barn was just an idea for the future, before they were even married, Cassie and Chad both wanted to take in homeless horses. There were so many of them that they also made a pact not to breed horses because they did not want to add to the numbers of them with no homes. Their only exception to that was if they received a rescued mare that was already pregnant. Phoebe had given birth to Reuben seven months after they had rescued her. He was a nice added surprise when they found out she was already in foal.

Cassie wondered if the new mare would be in foal. She and Chad would be short a stall in about a year if that was the case. But they had already planned to add on to the small barn. They were in the process of buying 30 acres of pasture adjacent to their farm so there would be plenty of room for horses to graze, run and relax. They wanted to give even more horses the chance to have a loving permanent home where they were safe.

Cassie called Chad at work. He was a software engineer for a large company. His high salary allowed Cassie to stay at home on the farm. She was self-employed as a book editor. She was also writing her first novel with a rescued horse as the main character. They also had a tiny house that they rented out for vacationers.

"Hey Cass! What's up?" Chad asked when she called.

"We got the mare!"

"Yay!"

"Do you want to go over to DJ and Hans' after work to pick her up?"

"I think I can get off work early today. We can go as soon as I get home – about 3pm."

"Okay, Chad, I will get the two - horse ready and hooked up."

"See you then, Baby!" Chad was as excited as Cassie about saving the new mare.

Cassie got everything ready. She had a new leather halter and lead rope for the mare. She filled a hay net and put it in the trailer. The Sanctuary was about an hour away and she wanted to keep the mare occupied so she would not be so stressed. Cassie knew she had been through a lot of trauma. She also called DJ to ask her if she should being Otis. DJ thought it would be a good idea. Otis had proven himself as a soothing companion animal for nervous horses. If the mare did not like him he could stay at the Sanctuary temporarily.

Cassie packed some bottled water and protein bars for the trip. Chad got home at 2:45pm. By 3pm Otis was in the trailer and ready to go. The drive to DJ and Hans' was uneventful. They had gotten on the road before the worst of rush hour traffic.

As soon as Chad and Cassie set eyes on the mare at the Sanctuary they felt relieved that she was safe and going home with them. She showed no objections to Otis and entered the trailer without hesitating. The four of them headed back to the farm.

On the way home Chad asked, "What are we going to name her?" He had chosen Rueben's name so it was Cassie's turn.

"I like the name Phoenix. She has risen out of the ashes and has a new life with us," Cassie explained.

"I like that," Chad responded with a grin.

"Then it is settled." Cassie smiled back at Chad.

They were in agreement about a lot of things in life. It made their mission to save horses a lot more enjoyable. And it helped during the rough patches that every marriage goes through. They both knew that no matter what happened they could count on each other.

Back at the farm they unloaded Phoenix. Otis unloaded himself and went back to his normal routine. Cassie walked Phoenix to the smallest of the three pastures away from the other horses in case she had brought anything contagious with her. Near the gate there was a shed, open on one side so she could go in to get out of the heat or rain when she wanted. There was whinnying back and forth between Phoenix and the other horses. After a while the boisterous horses settled down to graze quietly in their respective fields.

The veterinarian came out to check Phoenix a few days after her arrival. She still needed to gain a lot of weight and her coat was still dull from malnutrition. There was no indication that she was in foal. She seemed to be getting healthier already as far as Chad and Cassie themselves could tell. There was a slight noticeable difference from the first time they saw her. And she seemed more relaxed and content.

Over the next few weeks Chad and Cassie worked on expanding the barn. The purchase of the additional 30 acres was finalized and they were anxious to be ready for several more rescued horses.

In the meantime Cassie did some groundwork with Phoenix. She was not sure if the mare had been ridden before so she started slowly with the basics. Phoenix responded well. With Chad's help Cassie also introduced her to the herd. And after some minor pecking order issues they all settled into a peaceful cohesive group. Otis seemed to favor Phoenix and he grazed right beside her a lot of the time.

Cassie and Chad fell in love with Phoenix. They were so thankful that they were able to save her. They enjoyed sitting on the back porch at the end of a long day of working and finishing the barn just to watch Phoenix and the other horses graze in the waning sunlight. The contentment their rescued animals shared made all of their hard work more than worth it.

One early Saturday morning Chad and Cassie watched the horses from their bedroom window as the dawn slowly swept across the fields. The horses and Otis grazed as Chad and Cassie drank their first cups of coffee for the day. As he took a sip something else moved and caught Chad's eye.

"Look over there," he said pointing toward the other side of the field. "Deer!"

"Oh! A doe with twin fawns," Cassie said. "How sweet!"

Chad got the binoculars from the top of the bureau where they kept them for just such occasions. He gave them to Cassie so she could use them first. She looked at the deer through them for a few seconds and handed them back to Chad. He looked at the deer and then switched to the horses. Then something else caught his eye. Phoenix was limping.

"Cassie, look at Phoenix," he said handing the binoculars back to her.

"Oh, no. That doesn't look good."

Chad was already changing into jeans and a paint stained work shirt. "I'll go down and bring them all in so we can take a look at her."

"I'll get dressed and be right there." As Chad walked quickly down the stairs Cassie put on her own jeans and work shirt.

Chad grabbed a pastry from the kitchen and went to the barn to put sweet feed in each stall. The horses heard the sounds of breakfast and came in. Otis followed the slowly limping Phoenix into her stall. Mack and Pete headed to their food bowls where Chad was filling them too.

Cassie walked into the barn finishing half of a bagel with cream cheese and gulping down some apple juice. She handed Chad a second mug of coffee.

Phoenix quickly finished her sweet feed and stood nibbling hay left from the night before. Cassie put her halter on and gently led her out of the stall. She closed Otis in the stall so they could get a good look at how Phoenix limped while she tried to walk.

"She is almost walking three legged," Chad observed.

"Yes, something is wrong with her right front leg."

Cassie held Phoenix while Chad ran his hand down her leg checking for injuries, heat, swelling and painful areas. Her foot was warm. He checked her other feet for comparison.

"Feel this, Cass."

She felt the heat in the mare's foot too. "I'll call the vet's office."

Cassie knew there were several veterinarians in the practice they used and they made barn calls on Saturdays in rotation. That was one of the reasons Chad and Cassie had picked them for veterinary services. She went to the house where it was quieter to make the call.

Chad stayed in the barn. He brushed Phoenix and put her back in the stall with Otis. He gave them some more hay and opened the stall doors of the other horses so they could get back to grazing while he waited for Cassie to come back out. Then he started cleaning stalls and thinking about the logistics of how they were going to add more fences for the additional acreage.

Minutes later Cassie returned to the barn. "Dr. Jones will be here this afternoon around 2pm."

"Good deal. I'm going to clean up the barn and work on the addition for a while."

"I will join you," Cassie said as she took a pitchfork off of a hook on the wall and took it to a stall along with a wheelbarrow.

They worked until lunch then decided to take a break until Dr. Jones arrived. They ate and talked about Chad's ideas for the new fences, weighing the pros and cons of various configurations, keeping in mind the need for efficiency when moving horses in and out of the barn and the different fields.

After lunch they went out to sit in the swing on the front porch so they could see Dr. Jones arrive. Cassie played solitaire on her phone while they continued to talk. Chad watched the entrance to the farm. He had already walked down to open the gate before lunch.

Dr. Jones arrived at 2pm sharp. Chad jogged down to the barn and got Phoenix out of her stall. Otis was locked in the stall again for the visit. The mare was going to need him later one way or the other. He bleated once and went back to chewing hay.

The veterinarian examined Phoenix. She felt the heat in her foot and used her hoof testers. Phoenix reacted in pain.

After further examination Dr. Jones said it was an abscess. She gave the mare an injection to ease the pain. She gave Chad and Cassie antibiotics and pain medication with dosage instructions. She told them to call if Phoenix did not improve in the next ten days and they set up a time for her to come back for a follow up exam.

Cassie asked Dr. Jones if Phoenix should be kept in her stall. The veterinarian said that there were differing opinions about that and suggested putting her in a field without other horses. And Otis was welcome to stay with her.

After the veterinarian left Chad took Phoenix slowly out to the field. Cassie opened the stall door so Otis could follow them, then she made a chart for Phoenix's medications and pinned it on the bulletin board out in the barn. She and Chad worked on the addition a little while longer and then both took showers to get ready to meet their next guests arriving at the tiny house for a few days of relaxation.

Cassie continued to give Phoenix her medications over the next ten days. Her pain level, heat in her hoof and limping had not improved as far as Chad and Cassie could tell. So Cassie called the clinic to see if Dr. Jones could come out again. She was available the next morning.

Cassie got up early. Chad had already left for work. She went out to bring in Phoenix and Otis. She locked them in the stall before she set up feed and let the other horses in. They were waiting by the gate, all of them nickering except for the pony Owen who impatiently banged on the gate with his hoof. He did not need more than a handful of sweet feed and he did not want to miss breakfast. Cassie opened the gate and they all headed for the barn and into their stalls. She latched the stall doors behind them. After they ate she turned them all out except Phoenix and Otis. Mack and Pete ate their dog food and followed the horses back out.

Cassie went to the house for a cup of coffee and her own breakfast before Dr. Jones arrived. She was cleaning up the dishes when the receptionist at the clinic called and said the vet would be there in ten minutes. Cassie headed back to the barn and had Phoenix ready when Dr. Jones walked in.

She examined Phoenix and everything seemed the same except now there was heat in her left front foot too. Dr. Jones used her hoof testers. The pain was almost as bad as the right foot. She gave Cassie stronger antibiotics and altered instructions for how to treat Phoenix for the next week. They agreed that the veterinarian would come back at the end of that round of antibiotics. She was more concerned because the first round did not work. She also expected side effects that the new antibiotics could cause. She told Cassie what to watch for.

After Dr. Jones left Cassie called Chad to give him the update while she sipped another cup of coffee. They were both concerned and decided to just take it one day at a time until Dr. Jones came back. They both thought there was no sense in worrying in the meantime.

Their work on the barn continued. The shell was up and the roof was on so they started finishing the interior. And they finalized the plans for the new fences. Cassie had just finished editing a book for another author and did not have another one lined up yet so she took on the challenge of getting estimates from fencing companies. She also spent time working on her own book when she could squeeze it in for short spurts while taking care of Phoenix and everything else on the farm.

Over the next week Phoenix still did not get any better. If anything she seemed to be getting worse. And she experienced some of the side effects Dr. Jones had talked about. Chad and Cassie began to worry.

Dr. Jones came for the scheduled appointment. Chad had taken the morning off so he could be there too. He held Phoenix while the veterinarian worked.

"The infection in her feet is worse even though we have done everything that is supposed to work," Dr. Jones said. "We are running out of options for treatment."

"What is the next step?" Chad asked as he and Cassie looked to Dr. Jones hoping for a solution.

"There is one more antibiotic we can try."

Cassie said, "Let's go for it. I don't want to give up on her." Chad agreed.

Dr. Jones gave them the new antibiotics along with more instructions. She thought to herself that there was a low probability that this would work. Phoenix had been so run down and through so much trauma before Cassie and Chad had rescued her.

"I cannot promise that this will be effective," she said. "Phoenix still has a long way to go with her overall health. And this is one of those infections that has not responded to traditional antibiotics."

"We want to do everything we can for her," Cassie said. "We have only had her for a few months and we love her so much."

"We want what is best for her," Chad added.

"Let's give this new antibiotic a couple of weeks to work. I'll come out to check her in one week to see if there is any improvement." Dr. Jones gathered her supplies and once again left Cassie and Chad to care for Phoenix.

They wanted to maintain hope that Phoenix would completely recover. She was safe in their care and they wanted her to be healthy and pain free so she could enjoy life at their farm. They did not want any of their rescued horses to suffer.

A week later Dr. Jones returned. Phoenix was not any better and she was not any worse either. Chad was tied up in a meeting at work that day. Cassie and the veterinarian decided to give the antibiotics a few more days to see if they would knock out the infection.

Those few days were long and disappointing for Chad and Cassie. Phoenix was in more pain. They knew before Dr. Jones came out that the antibiotics were not working. It looked like Phoenix was not going to recover. There was nothing more they could do for her. They talked about letting her go on to Heaven. They agreed to let Dr. Jones look at her one more time, hoping that there was another way to help her get better.

Cassie called Dr. Jones out to the farm. Chad took the day off of work so he could be there too. Once again they got Phoenix ready for the veterinarian. It was only a half hour before the appointment time and it seemed to take forever. They were filled with dread. Cassie tried to distract herself by playing solitaire on her phone. Chad tried to work on the newly enclosed area of the barn. Neither could brush away the sadness they were feeling.

Dr. Jones arrived on time as usual. Chad and Cassie told her what they were thinking and feeling regarding Phoenix. The vet thoroughly examined the poor mare. She softly told them there was nothing more she could do. Cassie started to cry. Chad put his arm around her. They both felt helpless. Then they made the decision they did not want to make. They had to send her on.

After it was over they buried her in the field that she had shared with Otis. Chad and Cassie felt sad and empty. Their main goal in life was to save horses and take good care of them – not bury them. They had tried so hard to save Phoenix. They were deeply disappointed that she was gone. They felt so horribly hurt.

They both went through the next weeks alternating between feeling sad and feeling numb. During those darkest days, hours and minutes, they worked on the barn. Phoenix was gone and that hurt beyond measure but their goals had not changed. Losing Phoenix drove both of them to carry on. There were more horses that needed to be saved.

Phoenix's empty stall was a constant reminder that she was gone. Cassie and Chad both caught themselves glancing inside and feeling a fresh wave of pain. Otis had gone back to the main herd of horses. It hurt to think that Phoenix did not need him anymore.

The next Sunday evening Chad quietly asked Cassie, "How do you feel about calling DJ and Hans to see if another horse needs a home?"

Cassie hugged him and with tears in her eyes she replied, "Yes, that empty stall is tugging at my heart strings."

"Mine too, Cassie. Mine too."

On Monday morning Cassie talked with DJ about what had happened to Phoenix and told her they wanted to rescue another horse.

"Hans and I are making another trip to get five more horses on Thursday. I will send you some pictures. Can you take more than one horse?"

"We can only take one right now. The barn isn't finished yet and the fencing company is six weeks behind with their schedule. As soon as they are done we will let you know and we will take more horses."

Cassie and Chad made arrangements to pick up the new horse on Saturday. They had looked through the pictures that DJ had sent. A beautiful mare caught their attention. She was so thin and missing an eye. And they knew she was the one they were supposed to rescue this time. They decided to name her Pirate Girl.

On Saturday morning Otis once again loaded himself into the trailer. And once again they were off to save another horse.

Pirate Girl turned out to be a great addition to the farm family. Dr. Jones gave her a clean bill of health and scheduled surgery to repair the area around her missing eye. When she recovered she fit right into the herd. Otis decided to pair up with her as his grazing buddy and he lived in her stall. And as soon as the barn and fence were finished, Chad and Cassie rescued several more horses. They loved all of their horses and never, ever forgot Phoenix.

CHAPTER 9

GRIEVING THE LOSS OF YOUR HORSE AFTER A FIRE

Fire is one of the most devastating ways to lose a horse. Electrical fires can smolder for a while before anyone notices the smell of anything burning or sees any smoke. A lightning strike can occur even if it is not raining. And you feel so helpless to try to save your horse once a fire is out of control. You may not have time to evacuate every horse in the barn. Fires can happen even if

97

you do everything possible to prevent them. It is a sad fact of life in the world of horses

Corinne's Story

Corinne came from a well-known wealthy family and felt blessed to have the money to spend on her life's passion - horses. After college she travelled the world racing her Thoroughbreds. She often joked about not knowing where she was when she woke up in the morning because of her hectic schedule bouncing from time zone to time zone, racetrack to racetrack and one country to another for months at a time.

After several years of enjoying this whirlwind lifestyle Corinne decided to put down roots in her favorite place - the Commonwealth of Virginia. She found a real estate agent who specialized in horse farms and began her search for the perfect farm not too far from Washington, DC on the outskirts of Arlington, Virginia.

She searched patiently for a long time but could not find an existing horse farm with a home and barns that she liked so she settled for a beautiful 175 acre section of land with a small but acceptable house and some smaller out buildings. She hired an architect to draw plans for the barn and the house of her dreams. The barn would provide stalls for her horses as well as a number of boarded horses to generate some income. Further plans incorporated two riding arenas, one indoor and one outdoor, as well as several paddocks and three large pastures with open doorway sheds for horses to freely use. Corinne oversaw contractors and kept track of details. She had the money to spend and wanted the best facilities possible.

After several months and only a few delays due to weather, Wings of Grace Horse Farm opened for business. The buildings and grounds were attractive and soon Corinne had every available stall rented and started a waiting list of people who wanted to board their horses in such a beautiful setting. Corinne was happy with the farm and her boarders were happy to be there. There were trail rides and horse shows on the farm. It seemed like one big happy family.

Not long after the farm's one year anniversary things abruptly changed. It was not good. One morning Corinne's dogs awakened her early, barking in alarm. She jumped out of bed and hurried to the kitchen window to see why they were barking so frantically looking through the fence that surrounded the house. She took one look and panicked. The barn was on fire! And to make matters worse, it had been so chilly the previous evening that most of the horses were inside. She grabbed her cell phone and called 911 as she ran out to see what she could do until the fire fighters arrived.

Flames were everywhere in the barn. It was too hot to go in to save any horses. Corinne coughed in the smoky air as she grabbed a hose at the outside wash racks and sprayed the small part of the barn that it would reach. She felt so inadequate to accomplish extinguishing any part of the fire. When the fire trucks arrived she was quickly instructed to move to a safer place. She watched helplessly as the fire fighters did their best to control the fire. She soon realized that no horses in the barn could be saved. She was heartbroken and devastated. Nothing this bad had ever happened to her before.

The official investigation revealed that the fire started due to an electrical system mistake created during construction of the barn. It had passed inspection but the problem had not been detected because it was hidden in the framework of the building.

Since Corinne was from a well-known wealthy family her name was prominent in the local news about the fire and subsequent loss of horses belonging to her boarders as well as her own. Eager attorneys swooped down like vultures to pursue lawsuits on behalf of the other people whose horses had died. Not only did Corinne have to deal with grieving the loss of most of her own horses as well as those of her boarders, she also had to pay attorney fees and other costs associated with the lawsuits. All of the attorneys assumed that she had unlimited funds but her inheritance dried up under the endless onslaught of bills. It got to the point that she had to mortgage the farm.

Corinne had paid cash for her farm and building construction out of her inheritance. Rebuilding would use up all of the insurance money for the loss of the barn. She lost most of the income from the farm. Only a few of her broodmares in one of the fields were left. She had temporary stalls for them put in the indoor arena until the replacement barn was finished.

When Corinne rebuilt her barn she decided to switch her focus exclusively to breeding race horses and abandoned the idea of ever boarding horses again. The loss was too heartbreaking. Too many of the boarders were hurting and angry and she did not want to go through anything like that again. She felt responsible for the losses and pain they experienced even though she had done her best to hire reputable construction contractors to build the first barn. And her well known family name had made her a tempting target for potential future lawsuits. In spite of this she was able to move forward with her breeding business and the pain in her heart somewhat lessened.

When her barn was rebuilt, Corinne hired a consultant with fire prevention experience. She had a sprinkler system installed along with an alarm system that linked to her house so she could more quickly react to any potential fires in the future. She faithfully followed all of the advice the consultant had to offer and she prayed that this horrible situation would never happen again.

Preventing Fires from Happening

Barn fires and wild fires cause too many horse deaths each year. Fire is also one disaster that you can take measures to help prevent. There are so many fire hazards around our barns and ones created on fairgrounds and other places during horse shows and other events that could easily be avoided if people took the time to assess the risks and make good choices to eliminate them.

I attended a large international horse show in the Midwest several years ago and was astonished at what people were doing in the stall areas that could fuel fires and prevent people, horses and other animals from escaping in the event of an emergency. Some people had gone to great lengths to enclose their stalls with makeshift wooden roofs, walls, doors, and curtains. Furniture, including sofas, refrigerators, tables, lamps and cutains turned some stalls into lounges. The aisles were cluttered with horse paraphernalia. All of this stifled the flow of air and the stench of horse urine made me wonder how the poor horses could even breathe. It looked like one big fire trap. I could not help but wonder what were those people thinking! Why didn't show management have enforced rules about this? And how could this possibly meet fire codes?

Your barn may have fire hazards you do not know about. There are things you can do to eliminate many of those hazards. Although it is impossible to completely make your horse and barn completely fireproof, horse owners can take precautions to help prevent fires from starting in the first place. And just because your barn meets fire codes for your area does not make it fireproof. Those codes are just minimum standards and may be long outdated. Please go above and beyond your local and state fire codes to keep your horses, other animals and people safe. The list starting on the following page is not all inclusive but can give you a start on helping to prevent losing your horse in a fire.

Fire Prevention Tips

- Institute a "No Smoking Anywhere" policy for your property including electronic cigarettes. And if you board your horse at someone else's farm, make sure they do the same thing. Post 'No Smoking or Vaping" signs in strategic locations. State the consequences for that type of behavior. Tell boarders they must remove themselves and their horses from the premises immediately for the first offense. Use language to that effect in your boarding contracts. Underscore the seriousness of this problem.

- Ban box fans and any other fans not approved for agricultural use. Box fans designed for use in your home are not designed for horse barns. Dust can get inside the unsealed motors of those fans and cause a fire. Do not board your horse in a barn that uses home type box fans. If you are already boarding at a farm that uses them explain to the owner that they are fire hazards. They can be replaced with agricultural grade fans. And if you find that your agricultural grade fans get hot, replace them too. Also monitor, clean and maintain them on a regular basis.

- Ban heaters that are not designed and approved for agricultural use. Keep heaters monitored, clean and maintained. Disconnect them when they are not in use and when nobody is around to keep a sharp eye on them.

- Purchase fire extinguishers and place them in multiple locations inside and outside of your barn and storage buildings. Have them checked and maintained or replaced on a regular basis by someone who is an expert.

- Clean out cob webs and dust on a regular basis. They help fires spread faster.

- Store anything flammable such as hay and bedding in barns and sheds that do not house horses or other animals.

- Use electrical outlet covers to keep dust away from electrical wires that could cause a fire.

- Make sure any wiring in your barn is run through metal conduit to keep rodents from chewing it.

- Make sure any electrical work in your barn is performed by someone with the proper licensing in your area and passes any required inspections. And go further than code requires whenever you can to protect your horses and people.

- Know where the main gas and electrical switches are so you can cut them off if there is ever a fire. Post signs on them so others will also know where they are located in an emergency.

- Keep aisle ways swept or raked and free of anything that could be an obstacle when trying to escape a fire. This includes bedding, hay, tack trunks and saddle racks. Keep those items in a separate area or tack room.

- Keep the areas around your buildings free of brush, leaves, debris and junk piles, and keep the grass cut.

- Keep fire hydrants and water spigots clear of weeds and debris so they are easily visible to firefighters. This includes snow in the winter as well. Use reflective paint or tape on water spigots so they are visible at night.

- If there is not a fire hydrant close to your buildings consider having one installed on your property. They are expensive but may prove to be invaluable if there ever is a fire.

- Make sure your address is clearly marked at the road in reflective paint.

- Consider locating power lines underground during construction so firefighters can avoid logistical problems with their vehicles and equipment as well as minimizing problems with potential lightning strikes.

- Make sure fire trucks can navigate your driveway without large tree limbs, tractors, cars, horse trailers and other obstacles standing in the way.

- Make sure you have a fire evacuation plan for quickly getting your horses to safety if your farm is threatened by a wildfire or bad weather. Include the farm address, landmarks, GPS coordinates, and other identifying details to help firefighters find your home and barn.

- Post your fire evacuation plan in the tack room, break room, bathroom, hay barn, etc. used by anyone at the farm so they will see it on a regular basis. Make sure to check it to make any changes on a regular basis. And include a copy with every lease contract for boarders. And make sure they read, initial and sign it

- Make sure the road signs in your area are clear, visible and up to date. (Recently our neighbor's child was choking and emergency personnel stopped at our farm for directions because road signs were missing, confusing and inadequate all at the same time. They could not find the location of the house the child was in, wasting critical minutes in an emergency! Fortunately the child is fine now.)

- In case you are evacuated from your area due to a wildfire or other disaster, have a plan in place for your horses. Make arrangements with friends who have extra room at their farms in other areas just in case this happens at some point in the future. And have a plan in place of your friends need to evacuate to your farm too.

- If your horses survive a fire have them checked by a veterinarian even if they seem fine. Problems from smoke inhalation can show up at a later date and can lead to bacterial infections, other health problems and even death.

- Fire Prevention Checklist: Go to FireSafetyInBarns.com to find professional firefighter and equestrian Laurie Loveman's Fire Prevention Checklist for more important information to stop fires before they happen.

Use these fire prevention tips and the checklist at FireSafetyInBarns.com for your own barn, at horse show grounds, and please pass the information along to your family and friends who have horses. This list is not all inclusive. Please research other ways to prevent fires and talk with people at your insurance company.

CHAPTER 10

GRIEVING WHEN YOUR HORSE IS DIAGNOSED WITH CANCER

There is nothing more devastating than hearing that a loved one has cancer. It can be just as heartbreaking to find out your horse has cancer, especially if you have owned your horse for a while and have established a strong bond with her. You may find out a diagnosis early and have time to try any available treatments. You may find out when it is too late for anything to heal your horse.

Or there may be no cure at all yet. If your horse is diagnosed with cancer you may be in for a difficult season in your life like Eva and Joe in the following story.

Eva and Joe's Story
Eva finds a Lump on Jazzy

After lunch one unusually warm and beautiful late spring afternoon on her farm several miles outside of a small southern New England town, Eva decided to walk out to the barn to check on her horses and get ready for a quiet ride through the cool forest. She made sure she grabbed her cell phone just in case she needed it because she was riding alone. Her husband Joe was out of town on a business trip and would not be home until later.

Before grooming and saddling her older reliable gelding Gabriel, she checked on two of her broodmares and growing foals. Both were a few weeks away from being ready to wean. She glanced at Gabriel on her way to look at her prized three year old Jazzy. Gabriel munched contentedly on the alfalfa hay Eva had earlier placed in his stall for lunch.

When Eva looked at Jazzy eating her hay she saw a strange lump on her neck that she had not noticed before. She quickly brushed aside any thoughts of riding Gabriel and entered Jazzy's stall to take a better look. She felt around her throatlatch and winced at the size of the lump she had found. It must be some kind of a cyst, she thought. She wanted to make sure it was not something serious so she pulled her phone out of her pocket to call Dr. Keaton's office.

Anna Keaton had been Joe and Eva's favorite veterinarian for several years, caring for Gabriel, the broodmares and foals, and had seen Jazzy for the first time the day she was born a little over three years earlier. Her birth was textbook normal and Dr. Keaton had pronounced her healthy and told Eva and Joe that the filly would thrive in their care at their well-kept farm.

After calling the veterinarian, Eva groomed Jazzy so she would be presentable when Dr. Keaton arrived. She also cleaned the mare's stall. Then she groomed Gabriel and one of the broodmares trying to stay calm and productive while she waited.

A couple of hours after Eva's call to her office Dr. Keaton drove down the gravel lane leading to the barn. Greeted by the concerned look on Eva's face, she quickly walked through the door into the aisle way where Jazzy stood patiently waiting in crossties. Eva had quickly placed her there as soon as she saw the vet truck turn in from the road.

Dr. Keaton examined Jazzy, palpating the lump that Eva had seen and then checked for others. She frowned to herself in dismay as she felt another hidden lump on Jazzy's chest just above her forearms. It was not large enough to see but nonetheless disheartening. Anna checked her emotions and examined the young mare thoroughly, finding nothing else to cause concern.

As she finished looking for further symptoms, she turned to Eva and told her about the additional lump. Eva grimaced, not liking this at all. Anna calmly stated that she would need to biopsy both areas to find the cause. Without hesitation Eva agreed to the procedure. Anna told her that it could take two weeks to get the results and there was a possibility that it might be something serious although it could be nothing to worry about at all. She tried to reassure Eva that she would do everything she could to expedite the process and get back to her as soon as she possibly could with the results.

After Dr. Keaton drove away with the tissue samples, Eva felt frightened for Jazzy. She carefully returned the young mare to her freshly cleaned stall, checked her hay and her water bucket, and closed the back door leading to the pasture to keep her quiet and safe until she healed from the biopsy incisions.

While she walked slowly back to the house, Eva called Joe to let him know what was happening. His current business trip wrapped up that day and he flew home in the evening. Eva met him at the front door and they hugged each other tight. She and Joe loved their horses and it hurt both of them that something might be seriously wrong with Jazzy. And waiting for the results seemed to take forever.

Eva and Joe took turns checking on Jazzy. The small incisions healed quickly so they decided to open her door to the pasture. Jazzy seemed happy to get out of confinement. She nickered to the other horses and trotted over to graze with them, settling down close to Gabriel who grazed methodically on the other side of the fence.

The Biopsy Results

Several days after Jazzy had her freedom back Dr. Keaton called. She asked if she could stop by the farm later that day to check on Jazzy and talk about the results with Joe and Eva. At this point Anna left the words unspoken that the diagnosis was cancer. She dreaded the conversation they would have and she wanted to tell them both in person.

Joe and Eva went out to the barn a little while before Dr. Keaton was scheduled to arrive. Joe coaxed Jazzy inside with a handful of sweet feed as Eva grabbed her grooming kit. Joe put the mare in crossties and Eva carefully brushed her and picked out her hoofs. Joe swept up some scattered hay and poplar shavings in the barn aisle. Both worried and the chores gave them something else to focus on while waiting for the veterinarian.

They also distracted themselves by discussing their upcoming appointment with their farrier Justin, wanting to make sure all of their horses' feet were taken care of. One of the broodmares was getting over an abscess in her right front hoof that had been healing for a while. It was time for Justin to reevaluate her for soundness. It was easier to talk about that comparatively minor problem than to think of Jazzy and the unknowns of the situation with her.

Dr. Keaton pondered what she would say taking a deep breath as she pulled into the lane to the barn and stopped. She got out of the truck and went to the back to retrieve her veterinary kit. Joe and Eva greeted her there. They exchanged small talk as they walked into the barn. Anna examined Jazzy and found that her biopsy incisions were nicely healed and there were no additional lumps to be found. And the ones she had already found had not reappeared. That was somewhat encouraging. Anna still was not optimistic about any possibility of Jazzy's long term survival.

She asked Joe and Eva if there was someplace where they could sit down to go over the biopsy results. After turning Jazzy out into her paddock they somberly led the way to the back patio of the house where there were comfortable chairs and a table shaded by a huge umbrella. Joe arranged the chairs. Eva headed into the farmhouse to grab a pitcher of iced tea, some glasses and chocolate chip cookies she had made earlier from an old family recipe. Anna sat down, then organized and reviewed her papers while preparing herself to share the unwanted results. After the iced tea and cookies were served each of them prayed silently that Jazzy would get through this.

"Eva and Joe" Dr. Keaton began, "I really don't know how to say this." She hesitated a second as her voice wavered. "The biopsies show that, unfortunately, Jazzy has a type of cancer called Equine Cutaneous Lymphosarcoma. I am so sorry." There was a brief heavy silence.

Stunned, Joe and Eva both had tears in their eyes. They glanced at each other as Joe swallowed a lump in his throat and asked, "Is it curable?"

Dr. Keaton replied, "In some cases, if it is cutaneous – in the skin – treatment can possibly prolong life. That is the type of Lymphosarcoma that Jazzy has. Overall it is the most treatable and horses survive longer with that particular type of cancer but generally horses who have it eventually die from it. There is no cure available yet." Veterinary science was way behind on this front. She looked empathetically at Joe and Eva as they began to ask questions.

While an unchecked tear escaped down her cheek, Eva asked, "What treatments are there?" She hoped with all of her heart that something could be done.

Dr. Keaton went on to explain that there were several options including hormones, chemotherapy, medications and surgery. She added, "There is also the option not to treat her and just make sure she is comfortable for as long as possible with pain medications as needed. You can make this decision at any time during treatment. We will monitor her progress with blood work and examinations and other tests. Since you know Jazzy better than anyone you can tell if she is losing her appetite or weight, acting like she is in pain and any other changes."

Joe said, "Yes, this will have to be a team effort. And we have an emergency fund we can use for Jazzy's treatment. What is the best way to treat her and how much will it cost?"

Dr. Keaton gave them a lot of the details for each treatment and how they might be combined in different ways specific to Jazzy's needs. She explained that the overall costs would depend on how Jazzy responded.

"I will have my office manager give you itemized estimates before we make any decisions on how to proceed." She added, "It will be expensive so we will go over the procedures and the costs along the way to make sure there are no surprises and to see if you want to continue treatment. Again, we will monitor her closely. There will likely be good days and not so good days. We can adjust how we treat her as needed."

After answering more questions Dr. Keaton left to give Joe and Eva time to think about what they wanted to do with Jazzy. They both felt like they were facing a long hard battle to prolong her life. They walked back to the barn to pet Jazzy, feed her carrots and finish the rest of their barn chores. As they worked they intermittently took small breaks to talk about the options before them.

Two hours later, exhausted from the stress and their work, they closed the barn gate and headed to the house. They agreed to take a break from discussing Jazzy's situation until after showers and a quiet dinner at their favorite Mom and Pop restaurant in town.

The drive to Bailey's Bistro by the Bay was quiet with both Eva and Joe each lost in their own thoughts. Joe parked the car and they walked in. The hostess seated them in a booth back in a corner where they would not be disturbed. Neither of them was in the mood for chatting and pleasantries if anyone they knew might see them. It was all too much to deal with.

After ordering steaks along with Bailey's signature salads garnished with fresh blueberries and cherries served with the house secret drizzled dressing, they began to talk about anything they could think of except Jazzy. Eva praised the newly elected sheriff for the early success of her innovative plans to enforce the law and improve community relations. Joe shared some amusing stories that had happened during his most recent business trip to a city in the Midwest. They discussed future plans for their horse related YouTube channel avoiding mentioning Jazzy as one of the attractions viewers loved to see ever since they uploaded the first video of her the day she was born.

Later on the drive home Joe told more stories about his business trips, trying to distract Eva and himself from the painful challenges they were facing with Jazzy. Eve, deep in thought, did not respond.

"Eva, are you okay?" Joe asked softly. He did not want her to go through all of this pain. It was bad enough that he had to go through it too.

Tears slid down Eva's cheeks as she said, "No, this is not anything I expected would ever happen to us. All of our horses are special. We know they will eventually die but Jazzy is so young. It just breaks my heart!" She stifled a sob and stared out of the window into the fading light of the evening as the stars were beginning to appear.

Joe gently responded, "This is so painful for both of us. Maybe treatment will work."

"There is always hope," Eva said with a tentative smile. "Even if the current treatments do not completely work, they could keep her alive long enough for any new medications to become available."

"Yes," Joe agreed. "There is hope and we can try anything Dr. Keaton recommends. We have the money to pay for it in the emergency account. And between the business, which is doing quite well this year, and income from the Youtube channel, we should be able to handle the financial challenges."

When they arrived back at the farm they passed the house and went straight to the barn to check on Jazzy and the other horses again. All of them were in their paddocks except Gabriel who was asleep in his stall. They turned on the outside lights so they could see to walk out to the horses.

Joe and Eva headed to Jazzy's paddock where she greeted them with a low whinny as her ears perked up when she saw the scoop of sweet feed Eva had brought from the grain bin. They petted the mare for a few moments. When the sweet feed was gone Jazzy ambled away to nibble on some grass. They walked around to each horse to make sure they were all okay then took the car back to the house.

Joe drove into the garage. Exiting the car they walked through the door into the kitchen. Eva poured soft drinks and made popcorn as Joe fed and watered the dogs and cat. They met in the den, sat next to each other in the double recliner and silently hugged each other for a while.

Eva spoke first. "Neither one of us has ever been through anything like this before. Everyone in our family has always been healthy. All of our grandparents are still living. The only experience we have to go on is losing two of our dogs that died of old age."

"This is all new, uncharted territory for both of us," Joe said in agreement. "We have to take it one day and one decision at a time."

"I want to be proactive. I would like to research this disease and see what information is available out there. There may be something we can do that Dr. Keaton has not talked about yet." Eva wanted to fight, to attack the cancer with everything possible.

Joe felt the same way. "Honey, you and I are on the same page. How do you feel about calling Dr. Keaton tomorrow morning to see what is the first step to help Jazzy?"

"Yes," Eva said with renewed strength and resolve in her voice. "Let's do it!"

That night neither one of them could sleep. The stress was overwhelming. They both gave up by 2:30 am. Eva grabbed the remote off of her nightstand and turned on the television. Nothing on cable interested either of them. So Joe reached for the Roku remote on his nightstand and pulled up YouTube. They agreed that they needed to watch something soothing as well as interesting so Joe clicked on the Bob Ross channel. They both had been fascinated with Bob Ross's painting shows since they were kids. They watched multiple episodes until they both drifted off to sleep. Bob Ross painted on.

Decisions for Treating Jazzy

Eva woke up first, turned off the TV and went to the kitchen to get a cup of coffee. Joe soon joined her. They shared the morning barn chores, feeding and watering, letting horses out to graze and checking on Jazzy several times in the process. Since both worked from home they busied themselves on their laptops while watching the morning news until 9 am when Dr. Keaton's office opened. Joe set his cell phone on speaker as they made the call together. Dr. Keaton had alerted her receptionist Taylor that they would probably call. She immediately transferred the call to the veterinarian.

"This is Dr. Keaton," Anna said when she picked up the phone.

"This is Joe and Eva," Joe responded quickly. "We have made the decision to treat Jazzy - to give her a chance."

"Good. We can start treatment this afternoon if that will work for you."

"That is good for us. We will both be here," Eva said.

Dr. Keaton said, "My office manager Glenda should have a breakdown of the costs. We can go over that together when I come out to the farm today."

"That sounds good so we can keep track," Joe replied.

"We will see you this afternoon," Eva added.

Eva sat down to look at her laptop. She began to research Equine Cutaneous Lymphosarcoma. There were several veterinary web sites that only had minimal information. What little she could find was decades old. The trail ended there. She sighed. This is not encouraging, she thought to herself. Once again tears welled up in her eyes. She had to get her mind off of it. She busied herself editing a couple of videos getting them ready to upload on their YouTube channel, and writing a couple of blog entries to post on their web site in the next couple of weeks.

Joe had left to run some errands after the phone call with Dr. Keaton and came home with lunch for Eva and himself from a local sandwich shop. Eva had asked for a vegetarian sandwich since they had eaten steaks the night before. Joe had a meatball sub. They both drank cranberry juice.

While eating they talked about the dearth of information Eva had found. Why was there so little of it available? It seemed that nothing useful was being done to combat this horrid disease. They felt discouraged and helpless. Their conversation was interrupted by a phone call from Taylor at Dr. Keaton's office. The veterinarian was on her way to the farm.

In a few minutes Anna turned her truck into the drive and parked in her usual spot. The sky was overcast and it started to sprinkle. Joe waved her up to the house where they sat down at the kitchen table to talk about Jazzy. Eva had her customary chocolate chip cookies and a fresh pot of coffee ready along with organic sugar and hazelnut creamer.

Dr. Keaton explained several options to treat Jazzy including surgically removing the two known tumors as well as chemotherapy and other medications. She went over the possible costs for each one. She explained side effects and other challenges that could result.

"There is one other option that may help and it is a longshot. Progesterone can sometimes be helpful to a greater or lesser degree of effectiveness. The best way to do that is through pregnancy." Dr. Keaton took a breath. She was not sure how Joe and Eva would respond to something so out of the norm for treatment.

"Pregnancy?" Joe and Eva exclaimed simultaneously, as they exchanged looks of incredulity.

"Yes," Dr. Keaton replied. "As strange as that sounds it might reduce the size of, or eliminate, any tumors. We would have to check the biopsied tissue to see if the tumors are the type that has receptors for progesterone. If that is the case, breeding Jazzy might help if she can conceive."

Eva said, "Before this situation came up we had thought about breeding her at some point in the future. Friends of ours have a stallion we thought might make a good match." Joe nodded in agreement.

"I will call the lab to order the tests," Anna said. "Let's go out and have a look at Jazzy to see how she is doing."

The sun was back out so they walked to the barn without any need for an umbrella. Dr. Keaton gently examined Jazzy. There were no changes. She opted to postpone giving her any medications until the test results were back. She told Eva and Joe that she would see if she could have the tests expedited so that they could breed Jazzy as soon as possible – if the tumors had progesterone receptors.

The three of them chatted for a while. Then Anna left. Joe and Eva walked back up to the house to finish some work and figure out what to fix for dinner.

Later after eating, Eva and Joe called their friends Ryan and Kristen to let them know what was going on with Jazzy and to ask them if they could breed her with their stallion Chipster – barring unwanted results from the new tests. Ryan and Kristen empathized with them and heartily agreed to the possibility of the breeding.

Kristen offered, "Chipster is a good choice because he is so gentle. And his bloodlines will complement Jazzy's."

Ryan added, "We can take her whenever she is ready if you get the go ahead – WHEN you get the go ahead. I am optimistic that it will happen." Ryan had always had a heart for encouraging people.

"Thank you," Eva said breathing a sigh of relief that they were doing something to help Jazzy.

"You guys are the best," Joe added. "We will call you as soon as we know something."

Waiting for the test results was nerve-racking. The emotional roller coaster Eva and Joe were on felt like a never ending trap. When Dr. Keaton called they did not know if they would feel optimistic or devastated. She got right to the point.

"The tumors do have progesterone receptors. Take Jazzy to the breeder." She sounded cautiously optimistic as they discussed more details. "This may or may not help. I encourage you to go ahead if you agree."

Somewhat relieved, Joe and Eva thanked Anna and then called Ryan and Kristen to give them the news and arrange a time to trailer Jazzy to their farm. She was due to come in heat in the next few days and they did not want to waste any time.

Taking Jazzy to Rysten Farm

The next morning Joe hitched up the green and yellow horse trailer to the matching green truck while Eva put Jazzy's leather halter on along with her head bumper. She then wrapped her legs and put a light sheet on the mare. The wraps and sheet matched the colors of the truck and trailer.

Eva loaded Jazzy into the trailer. Joe lifted the ramp and locked it in place for the ride. Eva attached the mare's halter to the trailer safety tie and escaped out the side door. Jazzy busied herself munching a mix of timothy and clover hay. She had travelled to enough horse shows that it was just another relaxing ride with something good to eat along the way.

Joe easily stepped into the driver's seat of the truck. Eva hopped up to ride shotgun. They both fastened their seatbelts. Joe put the truck in gear and slowly accelerated to give Jazzy a smooth ride. Eva grabbed her phone to let Ryan and Kristen know that they were on the way.

Thirty minutes later the truck and trailer turned into the narrow lane leading to Rysten Farm. Ryan met them at the barn.

Kristen, a radiologist, was in the house reviewing CAT scans relayed through the internet from the area medical center ER. She finished her reports and joined them after they unloaded Jazzy from the trailer. Joe and Ryan locked up the ramp. Eva and Kristen removed Jazzy's leg wraps and sheet, then took her to a freshly cleaned stall. Jazzy sniffed at the water bucket and took a good swallow then headed out the back door to graze in the spacious rich green paddock.

Joe and Eva went over to Chipster's paddock on the other side of the barn to admire him. Many of his progeny had sweet temperaments and performed well at horse shows. They felt grateful that they had the opportunity to breed Jazzy with him.

Joe and Eva took one last look at Jazzy before going home. She seemed content to be at Rysten Farm. They knew they were leaving her in good hands with Ryan and Kristen. And Dr. Keaton would be there often to monitor her health, adjust medications and most importantly check for pregnancy. Since all of these concerns were covered they decided to go away for a few days to decompress.

Joe and Eva Take a Break

As soon as they arrived home from Ryan and Kristen's place, Eva called Taylor at Dr. Keaton's office. She had taken care of the animals and the farm before when they were out of town. She agreed to stay at the farm while Joe and Eva were gone. They prepared the guest room for her and Eva made sure the fridge and pantry were stocked with food they knew she liked.

Joe used their credit card miles to book a flight to Mobile, Alabama. From there they rented a car and drove to Orange Beach to stay in a condo. They were blessed to find one available with a balcony overlooking the ocean. They ate lunch at their favorite seafood restaurant. Then they went to the condo and unpacked. Exhausted they both took a nap.

Later they took a long walk on the beach and watched the sunset on the way back. It was good to get away and relax.

Several days later they flew home as rested and as ready as they possibly could be to face the long road ahead with Jazzy.

Jazzy in Foal and Surgery

The next few weeks were busy. Consultations with Dr. Keaton happened several times a week. Jazzy took her treatments in stride. Several weeks after they returned home from Orange Beach, Anna confirmed that Jazzy was pregnant. Elated, Joe and Eva brought her home. They called Dr. Keaton to let her know that Jazzy was back from Rysten Farm.

"Now that we know she is in foal and safely home it would be a good time to remove the tumors on her throatlatch and chest," explained Anna. "The one on her throatlatch is the most concerning because it could eventually interfere with breathing, eating and blood flow."

"It sounds scary," Eva replied. "And it sounds like the best choice." Joe was on board so they scheduled the surgery. That decision made sense to both of them now that Jazzy had more progesterone production to help fight the cancer.

Two days later Dr. Keaton performed the surgery. Jazzy had a few stitches on both places. Otherwise it went well. Jazzy's diet was adjusted as needed for a healthy pregnancy. Except for the healing surgical sites she looked beautiful. Dr. Keaton had not yet found any other tumors. Joe and Eva were more hopeful.

Fall and Winter

Summer waned and turned into fall. The air cooled along with the shorter daylight hours. Jazzy continued to do well. The baby inside her grew at a normal rate even in the face of all the medication. Eva and Joe prepared for the cold weather ahead. They bought enough hay to last until late spring. The storage barn was full including grain and poplar shavings for the stalls. All of their horses were set for the long winter to come.

Thanksgiving, Christmas and New Year's passed quickly. Joe and Eva enjoyed hosting large family gatherings at the farm with grandparents, parents, aunts and uncles, nieces and nephews. And there were friends in the mix including Ryan and Kristen.

The holidays gave way to the deep freeze of mid-winter. During the day the partially frozen green water buckets sat outside of the barn upside down in the sun to thaw and were quickly refilled with fresh water. The horses ran kicking up their heels, snorting small clouds of water vapor into the air. Old Gabriel was stiff and a little grumpy so Eva increased his supplements to help ease the pain. Jazzy gained weight as the foal grew in her belly.

Eva worked at home during the cold and snow. Joe flew back and forth to Florida on the weekends to film videos for the YouTube channel. They were doing a series of interviews with people who worked at horse shows, showcasing the roles they played along with glimpses of their personal lives on the show circuit – everyone from top trainers to blacksmiths to members of the show management teams. Eva edited videos as fast as Joe filmed them. In between Joe's business trips they narrated and collaborated on music and final touches before uploading and scheduling video releases on their channel. Subscriber numbers and product endorsements steadily increased. Several horse magazines interviewed Joe and Eva about their successes helping to ramp up business even more.

Money flowed into their bank account. Joe's business also continued to thrive. The increased income gave them more than enough to pay for Jazzy's veterinary bills. They did not need to touch their emergency fund or agonize over how to treat her with limited resources. They felt so blessed and grateful in that respect.

Naming Jazzy's Foal

Spring arrived later than usual with traces of winter's sloppy mud remaining. Jazzy was due to foal at the end of June. The other broodmares had already foaled by March. Those babies thrived. The yearlings had long since been weaned and occupied their own stalls. A couple of them were sold to new homes. Gabriel felt better as the weather warmed up. Eva took him for a quiet ride around the farm three or four times a week to loosen his stiff muscles and keep him in shape. He was not so grumpy about being ridden now that it was warmer outside and he actually seemed to enjoy the exercise.

Eva groomed Jazzy at least as often as she rode Gabriel that spring. She felt elated the day she first saw the foal move in Jazzy's belly. She called Joe to share the good news.

"I think we should celebrate," Joe said. "Would you like to go out to dinner tonight?"

"Of course! I cannot think of a better reason." Eva smiled.

This time they went to Bailey's Bistro by the Bay on a happy note. Jazzy's cancer seemed to be under control and her foal was healthy inside of her.

Between delicious bites of rosemary lemon chicken Eva asked, "How about picking out a name for the foal?"

Joe took a sip of sweet tea and replied, "That sounds good to me. Do you have any names in mind?" He took another bite of his savory rib eye steak.

"I am thinking about using some form of Jazzy's name. I looked up some names online today," said Eva. The one that got my attention is Jaazaniah. It means 'God hears me'. It sounds good for a filly or a colt."

"Jaazaniah," Joe rolled over his tongue. "I like that. It is different and sounds catchy. Let's go with that one."

Eva nodded as she reached her fork for another bite of chicken. "Yes, Jaazaniah it is then."

They finished their dinner with satisfaction and decided to share one serving of chocolate volcano mousse for dessert. That night they were both able to sleep in peaceful optimism in anticipation of the birth of Jaazaniah.

Jazzy's Foal is Born

As they waited for the foal to be born Joe and Eva made arrangements for Jazzy to be bred again to try to keep the cancer at bay. Ryan and Kristen agreed to another breeding with Chipster. They wanted to help Jazzy in any way they could.

The remaining weeks of Jazzy's pregnancy went by slowly and she foaled on June thirtieth, a little later than expected. Baby colt Jaazaniah looked like the perfect combination of Chipster and Jazzy. He also shared their sweet disposition. Joe and Eva recorded lots of videos of the mare and foal as he awkwardly adjusted to life outside of the womb in the first couple of days while getting used to using his gangly legs. Joe and Eva chuckled with delight as they watched him. Even though they had seen many foals go through those early days of life they never tired of seeing them.

Dr. Keaton soon cleared both Jazzy and Jaazaniah for a return trip to the stud farm for breeding. Early the next morning

Joe loaded Jazzy into the trailer and Jaazaniah followed her in without incident. Eva made sure the trailer's video camera was working and focused so they could keep a sharp eye on both mare and foal during the ride to Rysten Farm. Joe drove with even more care since the young foal was on board. Eva did not take her eyes off of young Jaazaniah, watching the video screen all the way to Ryan and Kristen's place.

Upon arrival Joe maneuvered the trailer, backing it up smoothly to the gate of the paddock that Jazzy and her baby would have to themselves. It was the safest place on Rysten Farm to unload young Jaazaniah after his first ride in the trailer. Ryan stood ready to help. Joe and he carefully lowered the ramp and opened the trailer gate so Jazzy and Jaazaniah could exit into the small field of grass. Eva took Jazzy out of the trailer, removed her leg wraps, head bumper and sheet, and then released her. She snorted and trotted off with her foal scampering behind her.

After watching for a few minutes, Eva and Joe headed home. They had a lot of work to do with Joe's business and a backlog of videos to narrate and edit for the YouTube channel. All of that kept them focused and consumed their time over the next few weeks when they were not caring for their other horses.

They visited Jazzy and Jaazaniah frequently and made more videos of them. The foal was thriving in spite of the medications he had been exposed to prior to birth as well as through Jazzy's milk. Things seemed to be going well.

Jazzy's Cancer Returns

Then one morning when Eva was busy uploading the videos she had finished editing, Dr. Keaton called. She asked if she could come over to talk with Joe and her.

Eva's heart sank. This could not be good. "Yes, Joe and I are both here today. What time would you like to come over?"

"I can probably be there in an hour if that will work for you," Anna said trying not to be emotional. Today's meeting would be worse than the day she first told Joe and Eva that Jazzy had cancer.

Eva hesitated, then with a lump in her throat she replied, "We will be here then. I will let Joe know." She turned off her phone and fought back tears as she walked over to the back door and opened it.

"Joe!" she shouted. He looked up from filling the water trough in the paddock closest to the house. "Dr. Keaton wants to come over to talk. She will be here in an hour."

Joe felt jolted by Eva's words. "I'll be up in a few minutes." He quickly gathered the water hose and turned off the spigot. After checking to make sure the gate was latched so Gabriel and two of the broodmares and foals could not escape he jogged up to the house.

When Joe walked through the kitchen door he found Eva sitting at the table with her head in her hands. "We'll get through this," Joe said gently. He tenderly ran his fingers through her hair to comfort her.

"There is no other choice," Eva responded as she stood to give him a hug. They stood clinging to each other in silence. The sounds of the ticking grandfather clock in the family room seemed strangely magnified. They walked outside to wait in the double swing on the patio.

When Dr. Keaton arrived they went inside to sit at the kitchen table once again. It was getting too warm to stay outside. The coolness of the air conditioning felt somewhat comforting at first.

They exchanged small talk as Anna arranged her papers. Eva poured glasses of lemonade freshly squeezed that morning. Joe grabbed a sack of donuts he had bought in town when he picked up a package at the post office earlier. He arranged them on a plate and offered them to Dr. Keaton and Eva. They each took a chocolate glazed donut and he took one with sprinkles. All three took a bite delaying for a moment the inevitable conversation.

Then Anna swallowed some lemonade, took a deep breath and began. "When I went to Rysten Farm this morning Jazzy's exam did not go well. And her blood numbers are off." She hesitated and looked at Joe and Eva.

"Are you saying that she is not pregnant?" Eva asked, hoping that was the only problem. Joe held her hand as they both looked at Dr. Keaton.

"The breeding did not take. Jazzy is not pregnant. I am so sorry."

Eva blurted out, "There is still time this year. We can try again!" There was fear in her eyes and voice.

"Her blood numbers indicate that there is something going

on in her liver. And I felt more tumors when I examined her this morning. They showed up on ultrasound as well. Unfortunately she is not well enough to try to breed her again."

Anna felt terrible giving Joe and Eva this news. Eva had tears escaping down her cheeks. Joe's eyes spilled over too. This was not fair, not fair at all.

She gently continued, "Jazzy has also lost a lot of weight in the past week." Again she hesitated. Joe and Eva sat in stunned silence. They both knew what she would say next. "Jazzy may only have a few more weeks to live."

Eva sobbed as Joe held her. Anna grabbed a box of tissues sitting on the counter, took one for herself and quietly passed the box over to Joe and Eva. They each took one.

"I am so sorry," Anna repeated as her voice cracked.

Joe tried to compose himself and asked, "What do we do now?"

Dr. Keaton said, "Bring Jazzy and her foal home. We will have to transition Jaazaniah from nursing to creep feeding with plant based milk pellets to keep him healthy. Jazzy can still nurse him as long as possible. We can start the transition with milk replacement formula that he can drink from a bucket, free choice. It will be a lot of work but it is the best solution for him. And we will help Jazzy to be as comfortable as possible."

Joe and Eva agreed. They felt so emotionally drained at the thought of losing Jazzy and they wanted the best care for both the mare and her foal.

Eva asked, "What can we do for Jazzy?"

Dr. Keaton answered, "Love her. We can give her medications for pain and other symptoms. We can take it day by day. I will come out every morning to see how she is doing. I will keep an eye on Jaazaniah as well to make sure he continues to thrive."

"Will he get cancer too?" Joe asked.

"It is not likely he would. It is not genetic."

Eva said, "That is good. We have to take good care of him."

Joe added "We can put Jazzy and her baby in a large field with Gabriel. He is so gentle around foals."

"Yes, that is a good idea," said Eva. "That will help Jaazaniah as he goes through this. We have a field already set up with a shed and creep feeder. There is enough room for all three of them to be comfortable."

Anna replied, "That sounds good. How about going to Rysten Farm to get them and bring them home this afternoon? It would be better for both of them to arrange that as soon as possible."

Joe said, "We can do that. First we need to move the other mares and foals out of Gabriel's field. And it is closest to the house so we can monitor Jazzy and Jaazaniah more closely."

Eva said, "I will call our feed supplier to order the milk replacer and pellets for Jaazaniah." She also called Ryan and Kristen to let them know what was going on and to set a time to pick up Jazzy and her foal.

Dr. Keaton left to finish her rounds at other horse farms in the area before heading back to her office for late afternoon appointments with small animals. As she continued the rest of her day she could not get her mind off of the anguishing situation so she prayed for Eva, Joe, Jazzy and her foal.

Bringing Jazzy and Her Foal Home

Joe and Eva went out to check all of the fields and to decide where to move some of the horses before they hitched up the trailer to bring home Jazzy and her baby. They had not eaten lunch yet so they fixed chicken salad on whole wheat bread to eat on the way. There was enough lemonade left to fill their bottles along with some ice. They also took the rest of the sack of donuts along with some baby carrots to share with Jazzy.

They finished eating just before they pulled into Rysten Farm. Even though they had visited Jazzy and Jaazaniah every couple of days they were still surprised at how big the foal had gotten once he followed Jazzy into the trailer. And they were shocked to see how thin Jazzy was and so suddenly. Reality was hitting hard.

Joe and Eva talked with Ryan and Kristen for a few minutes before they left. Both couples agreed to talk often through this difficult time. They exchanged hugs. Joe and Eva were grateful to have such good friends they could count on. They got back into the truck and took Jazzy and Jaazaniah home.

Back at the farm they unloaded the mare and foal in the field where Gabriel was. As expected the three horses were immediately comfortable with each other. Jaazaniah bounced around and Gabriel patiently watched him for a few minutes before joining Jazzy who was already busy grazing. In spite of losing so much weight she still had a good appetite.

The feed truck arrived the next day with Jaazaniah's milk replacer and pellets. He had been handled and groomed daily since birth and this made it easier to train him to adapt to eating and drinking his new diet. Eva brushed him and began to entice him to drink the milk replacement formula from a bucket in the creep feeder inside the shed. She also put a few pellets in the feed box there for him to try when he got curious. She replaced any uneaten pellets daily so they would not spoil.

Dr. Keaton stopped at Joe and Eva's farm every morning to check on Jazzy and her foal. For a few weeks Jazzy's condition seemed stable. Her blood numbers stayed the same. She lost a few more pounds but not at the rapid rate of the last week before they brought her home from Rysten Farm. Jaazaniah was still nursing and he was also getting used to drinking the milk replacer. He started nibbling at the pellets. Dr. Keaton was pleased that he was growing and doing so well. She said it was healthy for him to continue nursing as long as possible. And she felt relieved that

Gabriel was such a good companion for Jazzy and him.

Joe quietly decided to arrange for Jazzy's inevitable burial. One day when he left the farm to buy groceries he stopped by Jim's house on the next farm over. Jim had a backhoe and had helped other horse farm owners in the area. Joe gave him a heads up and he agreed to bury Jazzy. Joe felt relieved that they would not have to scramble when the time came. He kept it to himself not wanting to upset Eva. If she brought it up he would tell her.

Losing Jazzy

Another two weeks passed by. Eva checked on Jazzy right after lunch one day. She had seemed okay when Dr. Keaton came by that morning. Now she was suddenly and clearly in distress. Eva pulled out her cell phone and called the veterinarian. She was shaking and ran to the house where Joe was busy working on his laptop.

"Jazzy is in bad shape." Eva said with a trembling voice as she walked inside. "I already called Dr. Keaton. She is on her way over."

Joe got up from his chair and they quickly walked out to

see Jazzy. They both knew it was time to let her go – even before Dr. Keaton arrived.

Anna drove the fastest route she knew, still staying at the speed limit. As many times as she had faced this situation with people losing the animals they loved, it never got any easier for her. She always hoped and prayed that she could save a life against all odds. And sadly she knew it would not happen this time. Veterinarians have feelings too and this was the most difficult part of her job. The best she could hope for at this point was to be there as a friend who cared as well as a doctor. When she got to the farm she found Joe and Eva with Jazzy. She could see the hurt in their eyes.

Eva spoke first. "I can't stand Jazzy being in so much pain."

Dr. Keaton examined the beloved mare with a sinking heart. She knew there was nothing more she could do for her. She quietly asked Joe and Eva what they wanted to do, knowing in her heart and mind that they would make the right choice. Jazzy was suffering.

Eva replied, "This is too hard for her. She needs to go on. We cannot let her live like this." She looked tearfully at Joe to see what he would say. This was such a tough decision for both of them to have to make.

He agreed. "Yes, we think it is time to let her go." He had tears in his eyes too. Eva fought back sobs.

Dr. Keaton gently said, "I know this is so very difficult. I think you are making the right decision. Take your time to say goodbye to her."

While Eva stood next to Jazzy petting her Joe stepped away out of earshot, pulled out his cell phone and called Jim. Then he called Ryan and Kristen. All three of them got there as soon as they could. Kristen and Ryan had been through this before themselves and they wanted to be there for Joe and Eva.

Dr. Keaton quietly walked back to the truck to get her supplies and wait for Eva and Joe to get through these final sad moments with Jazzy. Jim did his preparations next to the field Jazzy had shared with Jaazaniah and Gabriel.

When it was over Eva and Joe walked slowly to the house with arms around each other. Both were crying. Kristen went with them. Joe had asked Ryan to lock Gabriel and Jaazaniah in the large run-in shed until Jim was finished. He stayed with them to make sure they were okay. Anna gathered her equipment, put it in the truck and went up to the house to comfort her friends.

After a while Dr. Keaton left to perform emergency surgery on a dog that had been hit by a car. He would survive and be fine. Ryan and Kristen called their assistant to ask him to feed their horses. They stayed to help feed Joe and Eva's horses and clean up the barn.

Joe went back out for a few minutes to check on Gabriel and Jaazaniah while Jim was still busy working. Eva stayed in the house. It was all too much.

Joe coaxed the foal back into the creep feeder area after preparing some fresh milk replacer and pellets. He fed Gabriel some sweet feed and a couple of flakes of hay. Jaazaniah seemed calm. Dr. Keaton had left some medication just in case he became distraught. After finishing Joe trudged back to the house. He needed to be with Eva. And she needed him too.

After the horses were all fed and in clean stalls or turned back out in their fields, Kristen left to pick up some take out dinner from Alexander's Greek Feast, a restaurant where she and Ryan had eaten multiple times with Joe and Eva. She brought the food back right after Jim had finished his work and gone home.

Ryan met her in the driveway to help carry the food into the house. He had just let Gabriel and Jaazaniah out to graze. The colt seemed to still be doing just fine, sticking close to Gabriel who grazed patiently next to his young frolicking buddy.

Walking into the house with the food, Ryan and Kristen found Joe and Eva sitting on the couch quietly holding each other. Kristen gently broke the silence, "I picked up some dinner." She and Ryan set the bags on the counter in the kitchen and started to unpack and arrange everything on the table.

"Thank you," said Joe and Eva simultaneously. They both got up from the couch to help. Joe got out plates and glasses and Eva put flatware and napkins on the table. Kristen had stopped by a convenience store on the way back to the farm and bought a gallon jug of Tipper's Sweet Tea flavored with oranges. She noticed oranges in a fruit bowl next to Joe and Eva's coffee maker and sliced one to add to the glasses of tea. Ryan put gyros on the plates and grabbed some bowls out of the cabinet for salads. There were brownies and baklava for dessert.

They all sat down to eat. Eva and Joe both ate slowly finding it difficult to enjoy the food yet both were grateful for Ryan and Kristen's generosity and friendship.

After a few bites, Joe said, "Eva and I have been talking off and on for a while about how to memorialize Jazzy."

Eva said, "We were shocked that there is so little to help Jazzy and other horses with cancer." A tear escaped her eye.

"We would like to start a fund to donate money to cancer research for horses," said Joe.

"And other animals too," Eva added. "We want to help as many as possible."

Ryan and Kristen quietly listened as they talked about some of the details they were considering.

"We can ask Dr. Keaton if she knows of any universities with veterinary schools doing research in that direction," Joe stated quietly.

"Yes, and we can do a series of videos about Jazzy on our Youtube channel as well as ask for donations." Eva seemed less sad for a few moments.

Kristen smiled softly. "That sounds good. We would like to help."

Ryan gently added, "Yes, I can talk to Henry at First Street Bank to set up an account to receive the donated money."

"And we can make the first donation," said Kristen. Seeing how fatigued both Joe and Eva looked she added, "You guys need to get some rest. I will clean up the kitchen so you can wind down for the evening and get some sleep."

Eva was too tired to argue with her friend. She went to the master suite to take a shower. Joe stayed in the kitchen to help with the cleanup. He and Ryan talked about sports to get their minds off of the sad events of the day. Kristen was thankful that they did.

When the kitchen was clean and in apple pie order, Kristen and Ryan, who were also fatigued from the day's events, went home after checking once again on Jaazaniah and Gabriel. Joe showered and followed Eva to bed and they hugged each other. They were both so emotionally drained and exhausted that they were able to sleep through the night in each other's arms.

Early the next morning Joe and Eva went together to check on and feed Jaazaniah and Gabriel. It was so sad and difficult to see them without Jazzy in the mix. It was not fair at all.

Finding Hope in the Midst of Grieving

Joe and Eva spent the next few days trying to focus on work and getting their lives back to normal amidst the aftermath of the loss of Jazzy. Jaazaniah was doing remarkably well even though his transition time from nursing to being weaned and losing his mother was so short. He had already bonded with Gabriel in the process and continued to thrive. The ever patient Gabriel was his hero. Joe and Eva felt relieved and grateful. They had a new appreciation for their older gelding.

A couple of weeks later Joe and Eva went to Ryan and Kristen's house for dinner. They planned to talk about their fundraising for animal cancer research. Dr. Anna Keaton joined them with her husband Steve. Farrier Justin Smith and his wife Audrey came to help too. Ryan had talked with his friend Henry at First Street Bank. He was onboard and ready to open an account, and he had already promised matching funds for the first donations with his own money. His family had lost a dog to cancer a couple of years before. The Keatons offered a second round of matching funds.

Reaching out to help other people whose horses and other animals also had cancer helped Joe and Eva through their journey in the grieving process. It became a lifelong passion for them.

They had more sad days than good days for a while as they grappled with losing Jazzy. Through the ups and downs they focused on giving hope to others faced with the same situation. And they found hope again with Jaazaniah who would one day sire Jazzy's grandbabies.

CHAPTER 11

GRIEVING WHEN THERE ARE OTHER FACTORS INVOLVED

Sometimes there are other factors making the loss of your horse even more complicated and worse, like what happened in Corinne's story in Chapter Nine. Other people involved might grieve along with you. You may have lost your horse in a fire, hurricane, tornado, flood, earthquake or other large scale disaster. Your horse may be lost or stolen and you have exhausted all avenues in an effort to find her. Losing a dearly loved horse may also become a huge financial blow to your breeding program, training, boarding or riding lesson business.

Roger's Story

Roger lost his stallion King and there were other factors involved in his situation. He taught fifth grade at the local school in a small close knit town in Indiana where there was only one classroom for each grade. He lived nearby on the horse farm passed down from his grandparents. He brought pictures and stories to school of his Paint stallion King, as well as the broodmares and foals on the farm to share with his students. King had consistently sired crops of foals with halter champions every breeding season for the last few years. He was still young and Roger had looked forward to many more of his offspring coming into the world. Breeding outside mares had brought in extra income to supplement his teacher's salary. His wife Leanne was physically disabled and stayed at home working in her part time business adding as much to their income as she could.

One day after work Roger went out to check on the horses and found King dead in his paddock. He had seemed fine that morning before Roger went to work at the school. Leanne was not able to leave the house to take care of the horses and did not know anything had happened to King until after Roger had found him. His death was a mystery. The veterinarian could not find any obvious cause. Roger and Leanne were devastated. To make matters worse Roger had used a lot of their savings to pay for King and had also let the mortality insurance on his stallion lapse.

Roger was going through anger at himself for losing so much money as well as grieving King's death. He felt pain from the future foals that would never be conceived because of this special stallion's death. And there was no money to replace him in the breeding program for the foreseeable future. Leanne was just as heartbroken about losing King but she did not get angry at Roger for losing so much of their savings and letting the insurance go. It might take years for them to get back to where they were with their finances. But they were both thankful to still be young enough to eventually rebuild their savings before retirement.

It broke Roger's heart to tell his students what had happened to King because he had shared so many stories with them about the young stallion and his adventures at the farm and horse shows. Many of them had shown a lot of interest in learning about King, and the mares and foals. Roger had included information about his horses in his classroom lessons for science, reading and English, finding clever ways to use them in teachable moments. Some of the children had visited King and the other horses at the farm. Now the students were learning about King's death and it was a sad time in that tiny town.

Eventually Roger replaced King with another young stallion gradually rebuilding his breeding program. And this time he made sure he paid his new stallion's mortality insurance and carefully pushed money back into the savings plan for the future.

Veronica's Story (Part Two)

And Veronica's grieving over losing her horse Lucy also included other factors. Veronica and her family lost their home and farm buildings in the tornado. They had to start all over again with their farm. They lost almost everything in their home. They were grateful to be able to recover some irreplaceable family photos that were caught in the trees around the farm and neighboring area. And they had the resources to rebuild their home and barns. They lived in a trailer for a while during rebuilding. It was a long slow recovery but they were able to get back to almost normal, although a different and new normal. And they are thankful that the family survived intact. When Veronica eventually bought another horse and resumed her riding lessons, it was never the same as having Lucy but her new mare Gabby turned out to be a blessing and a joy to ride. And the flaxen maned Gabby had previously been trained to pull a cart so Veronica was able to try driving and found a new activity she loved with her new horse. She still felt the pain of losing Lucy but she was more optimistic about life now that she had gone through a time of grieving and healing with her parents. They supported each other through the process and their dogs Cooper and Maggie helped them too. That was priceless to all three of them.

CHAPTER 12

GRIEVING WHEN YOUR HORSE IS LOST OR STOLEN

If your horse is lost or stolen your pain and anger can be excruciating. You have no control at all over these circumstances and that is a horribly helpless feeling. Either your horse has gotten loose and wandered away or some heartless thief has infiltrated your life and property long enough to take your prized horse, your best equine friend, without your permission and has gotten away without detection. You feel like you have been horribly violated.

The grieving process begins and in the midst of it you are trying to find your beloved horse, not knowing when or if you will ever see her alive and well again. Your heart aches as you search for him. You are angry and devastated, left with haunting unanswered questions. You may not be able to sleep or eat. You cannot concentrate on anything else. Your life has come to a screeching halt while you try your best to cope with this terrible situation and find your horse.

Tiffany's Story

Tiffany's Quarter Horse Beamer was missing from her Pennsylvania farm. After coming home late from work one unusually stormy day, she did not see Beamer when she went out to feed him. She had thought he would have taken refuge in the barn that was always open for him but he wasn't there.

She looked around the barn and then slogged through the large, sloppy wet pasture searching for what seemed like hours.

She finally found a break in the deteriorating old fence and her heart sank. Beamer was gone. He could have gotten out by himself or someone could have broken through the fence and taken him. It had happened in the middle of a day of raging, pouring thunderstorms and any distinguishable tracks had been washed away.

Tiffany chastised herself for not getting home from work on time and checking on him sooner and also for not making sure the fencing was in good repair. Her job seemed to have taken over her life lately and there was not much time for anything else, including Beamer.

Law enforcement officers found no evidence to go on. It was a mystery. After driving around for hours looking for him, Tiffany cried herself to sleep that night. She hoped and prayed that he would wander back to the farm on his own.

The next day Tiffany designed and printed posters and contacted everyone she knew to be on the lookout for a loose or stolen horse. She hoped that someone would recognize him by his unusual slanted blaze. She posted signs with Beamer's picture at the local show arena, tack shops and feed stores. She sent a letter with his picture to all of the equine veterinarians in the area. She posted the information on social media sites. She offered a reward for his safe return. She notified the local animal shelter in case someone had found him and turned him in.

Tiffany spent some time in the evening and on the weekends patching and rebuilding the old fence while an eternity of weeks went by and nothing happened with her heart driven quest to find Beamer. Weeks became months and the fence was long finished. Tiffany went through all of the phases of grieving Beamer - the shock, wondering why, and the anger at herself for not checking on him earlier that day, promising God she would be a better person if He would bring back Beamer. She thought about the possible reality that she would never find him. Her heart ached.

Even though she missed Beamer with all of her heart, she decided to buy another horse to ride until she found him. She searched until she found a suitable horse making sure her papers were in order and doing her best to make sure she was not missing from her home too. She brought Callie home and showed her in western pleasure and trail classes with Beamer constantly on her mind. Quietly she dedicated every horse show performance to him. And she displayed posters of Beamer on her trailer at every show and asked people if they had seen him. Nobody had. Tiffany and Callie collected a room full of ribbons, trophies and other prizes. Callie took her mind off of Beamer sometimes and for that she was grateful. All the while Tiffany continued to pray for Beamer's safe return.

Tiffany also rescued two dogs, Gracie and Peanut, from the local animal shelter to help keep her new horse safe from any bad guys who might be lurking around. They were both good at sounding the alarm anytime someone came onto the property. And life went on even though Beamer was still missing.

Two years later Tiffany received an unexpected phone call from her friend Rachel. She had been to a small horse show at a farm about fifty miles away that day. She saw a horse with a slanted blaze grazing in the pasture close to the riding ring. He looked a little thinner than she remembered but she thought it might possibly be Tiffany's lost horse. Rachel quickly texted a picture of the horse to Tiffany. As soon as she looked at it she knew for sure. It was Beamer!

Tiffany got directions from Rachel and immediately drove over to the farm. She took her friend Alvin who was in law enforcement just in case things got out of control in the confusion of what happened. Alvin dressed in regular clothing instead of his uniform so no one would be unnecessarily alarmed. Tiffany, along with Alvin, knocked on the door to the farmhouse and soon Jillian opened it. She welcomed them in and seemed so nice that

Tiffany's fears melted away and she felt comfortable telling Jillian about Beamer's disappearance.

Tiffany showed Beamer's registration papers and pictures to Jillian. It turned out that Jillian had bought Beamer with no papers a few weeks earlier at an auction. She even had a bill of sale. She thought he was just a really nice grade gelding and immediately fell in love with him. She had no idea that he belonged to someone else.

Jillian did some research through the auction company and found that prior to her purchase Beamer had been through a few owners. The trail ran cold and there was no concrete information on how he had left Tiffany's farm. The only thing they knew was that when or after he left Tiffany's farm some unidentified person had taken possession of him. Tiffany and Jillian never found out what had really happened.

Jillian was sad to see him go but she was thankful to be able to help Tiffany reunite with Beamer. Tiffany felt extremely grateful to have her favorite horse home again. Gracie and Peanut greeted him like he was an old friend. And she was pleased that Beamer and Callie became good pasture buddies. The horses and dogs settled into a peaceful routine.

Tiffany celebrated with friends and family and invited her new friend Jillian, who had already replaced Beamer with another gelding, to attend the party. Of course Tiffany invited Rachel to the party too. Thankful that she had found Beamer, she had offered her the reward she had set aside for whoever found him. Rachel refused to take it. She did not need the money and was just happy to have helped. Tiffany used part of the reward money to reimburse Jillian for the amount she had paid for Beamer.

Even though there was a happy ending to her long painful ordeal, Tiffany still had anxiety thinking about losing either one of her horses again. She decided to turn that anxious energy into something positive by launching a free web page to help people searching for their lost animals. Word spread quickly and within weeks the first horse was found, soon followed by the return of a missing dog. Tiffany was glad to help. And as a result she was invited to speak about her experience at meetings for horse people and other animal owners.

Actions to Help Get Your Horse Back

Try every resource you can think of to get your horse back including:

- Talk to local law enforcement and animal control officers.

- Print and hang posters at your area's feed and tack stores as well as veterinary clinics.

- Put ads in your local papers. Some will let you do that without charge.

- Talk with local radio news services.

- Talk with local TV and provide any video you may have featuring your horse so people get a good look at him, including his color, markings and the way he moves which can all be good clues that may catch someone's eye to help you find him. Even if they do not feature your story on the evening news the station might list it on their web site.

- Place the information on every social media web site you can find.

- Offer a reward for her safe return.

- Notify veterinarians, farriers and other horse professionals in your area to be on the lookout for your horse.

Sometimes Missing Horses are Found

Sometimes people do find their lost or stolen horses like Tiffany did. And there is tremendous relief and a happy reunion. It is such a blessing when that happens. You can resume life with your horse and be wiser and more alert to help prevent it from happening again in the future.

Sometimes Missing Horses are Not Found

On the other hand, your horse may be gone forever. You wait endlessly and nothing happens. You increase the amount of the reward and nothing happens. You wait some more. You feel so violated. Your life has been turned upside down. You may grieve your missing horse for the rest of your life. You may feel like you want to buy another horse. You may feel so heartbroken that you never want to buy one again. It hurts beyond belief.

The raw pain you feel is going to take a long time to diminish. It may never completely go away in this life. It is normal to grieve in this situation too. It is okay to be angry. It is normal not to trust people for a long time if your horse is stolen. At first you may feel that no one can be trusted. Your world has been turned upside down by a person who chose to hurt you by stealing your horse. Gradually you realize that there still are people you can trust. That takes time and is also a normal part of your grieving process when your horse is stolen.

CHAPTER 13

THEFT AND LOSS PREVENTION

Find and use all of the theft prevention resources you can to keep your horses from being stolen or lost. The following is a list of things you might do. It is not all-inclusive but it may help.

- Ask your veterinarian to microchip your horses even if they are not registered and their breeding is unknown because every horse you have is valuable. This gives you proof of identity as well as ownership.

- Another option is to have your horse tattooed on the inside of the upper lip. All Thoroughbred and other breeds of race horses are required to have this type of tattoo prior to the first race.

- Use motion detector lights around your barns and farmhouse to alert you of anything that may trigger them and possibly scare off bad actors.

- Set up video surveillance cameras that you can monitor even if you are not home. Make sure some cameras are hidden or high enough that they cannot be reached even with a pole. Research to find out which system will work best for your situation. Talk with other farm owners who already use video surveillance about different options that work well for them.

- Post signs warning bad actors that video cameras are present so they will be encouraged to move on without trying to steal your horse.

- Post No Trespassing and Beware of Dog signs. This may seem obvious but can also sometimes help when going after bad actors through legal means.

- Keep dogs to alert you when someone has entered your property and to scare off potential bad actors.

- Make sure your fences are sturdy and high enough to keep your horses contained. Inspect them on a regular basis and every time there has been bad weather. Make any necessary repairs right away.

- Install remote controlled electric gates to any access points on your farm that you can lock to keep trespassers out. Keep access points to a minimum. Use solar power if possible so that power outages will not cause vulnerability to horses escaping.

- Keep any gates on your property that you rarely access locked with heavy chains. This will make them harder to break into.

- Make sure electric fences are properly maintained and functioning. If the charger is not inside a barn or other building make sure it is sheltered from lightning strikes and other bad weather.

- Keep your eyes and ears open to what is happening regarding horse thefts in your area. There may be trends and patterns that you can watch for and guard against.

- If you board your horse at someone else's farm,   ask questions about their practices to help prevent theft. Encourage improvements in the farm's systems.

- Always have someone keeping an eye on your horses at shows and other events if you need to leave them even for a few seconds. Do not take any chances.

- When purchasing a horse, make sure to authenticate her papers and make sure they match your horse exactly down to every marking. Ask for proof of ownership. It may seem like an impolite thing to do but it may help prevent you from buying someone else's stolen horse. If the seller is reluctant to provide documentation, look at it as a red flag. Put the purchase on hold until you investigate and get the required information. If you have the horse vetted at purchase, make sure the veterinarian scans the horse for any microchip information.

- Find out what your state and local laws are for making sure lost or stolen horses do not end up in kill pens and slaughter houses.

- If the laws are inadequate or non-existent get involved to push legislation through to help protect all of our horses. Law enforcement personnel can only do so much with their limited resources. We ourselves have to take responsibility to make it as difficult as possible for heartless thieves to steal our horses.

☐ Horse Owners Need to Look Out For Each Other

Tiffany may have been able to get her horse back sooner if the people who had him after he disappeared had diligently insisted on proof of ownership and checked to see if a similar horse was lost or stolen. As responsible horse owners we need to look out for our horses and each other to make sure the bad guys are caught and discouraged from stealing horses.

CHAPTER 14

IS YOUR GRIEVING NORMAL?

It is Okay to Grieve

Losing a horse can be as traumatic as losing a family member or a close friend. It is normal to grieve. Each loss in your life will trigger the grieving process. Each time the process will be different from any others. There is no set period of time that you should be finished grieving. Depending on your individual circumstances you may go through the stages of grief quickly or it may take a long time. Your pain is your pain, so do not let yourself or anyone else put any expectations on you to finish grieving by a certain date.

And you may cycle through the phases of grief more than once. This may be triggered by the anniversary date of your horse's death or another sad event in your life as well as a happy event such as buying a new horse. That is normal. It is also normal to laugh when retelling a funny story about your horse even in the midst of crying. You do not have to feel guilty about that. It is normal.

Be Patient with Yourself

During the grieving process be patient with yourself. Try not to add extra stress by loading your schedule with tiring activities. Give yourself time. If you want to, talk to people in your life whom you trust about losing your horse. Talk to friends and family you can trust. Sometimes talking to a counselor, a pastor or life coach can help you walk this difficult journey. Sharing your grief with an understanding person can help relieve some of the pain.

If you open up to someone who does not understand your grief, walk away and talk to another person who does understand. Not everyone gets it that it hurts to lose an animal, especially people who are not interested in having pets of their own. They may say something insensitive like, "You can always get another horse." That does not help because any other horse, as wonderful and unique as it is, cannot truly replace the horse you lost. They may not understand that you can bond with a horse like you can with a person. They do not understand that horses are individuals just like people with their own personalities and other qualities. As painful as it can be, give those people some grace, walk away, and talk with someone else who does understand.

You may not feel like talking about it at all. That is okay as long as you are not stuffing the stress of grieving inside and holding onto it with an iron grip. Find another outlet to deal with the stress of grieving. Write in a journal if that appeals to you. Participate in exercise or sports. Volunteer your time in a charity either related or unrelated to grieving the loss of your horse like Joe and Eva did. You might consider fostering a horse that needs a home until a permanent home can be found. You can also do this to maybe to see if the horse is a good fit for you without yet making a long term commitment. Do something for you that helps you. If you try something that does not work, simply try something else.

CHAPTER 15

FAMILY MEMBERS EXPERIENCING THE GRIEF

Talk to your spouse and children, and other family members to see how they are doing during the grieving process. Even a child who has never shown any interest in horses can be quietly suffering the loss of your horse. As a parent you are the best person to observe your child's behavior and see the signs of grieving that no one else can see. Is your son having unusual outbursts of temper? Are your daughter's perfect grades slipping? Do they just want to stay home from school and have no interest in their other normal activities?

And your child may quietly worry about you as you go through this. Your child does not want you to feel this pain any more than you as a parent want your child to go through any heartache even though it is inevitable in life. Sometimes children may even think something like the death of a horse is their fault even though it had absolutely nothing to do with them. They may think that if you had not gone to their sports event or taken them to a movie that night you might have caught the problem before your horse died. Make sure your child understands that anything they did was not the cause of your horse's death and that you will be okay even though you are grieving.

Talk to your children about the grieving process in terms you know they will understand based on their personality, age and life experience. It may be the first time they have gone through the process of grieving after a death. Although painful, it can serve as a learning experience that will give them a foundation for dealing with the inevitable death of loved ones in the future. Tell them it is normal to cry and ask questions about death. Tell them it is okay to smile one minute and cry the next. And if you keep the lines of communication open, this can be an opportunity for your family to draw closer together.

CHAPTER 16

MAKING DECISIONS DURING THE GRIEVING PROCESS

You may feel tempted to make some big changes in your life in response to losing your horse. Try not to make any big decisions too soon. Do not pressure yourself or let anyone else pressure you into hastily buying another horse. Do not buy a new horse unless you know for sure that you are absolutely ready. If you have other horses do not make any big decisions about them such as selling any or all of them in your time of grieving. The biggest reason not to make major decisions is that you may regret it later when you are not feeling such intense pain from losing your horse.

If you receive an insurance settlement for the death of your horse put the money aside for a while so you have the time necessary to get through the grieving process and can decide later what to do with the money when you are not so overwhelmed.

Do not tell anyone if you get an insurance settlement. There are people out there who may not have your best interests at heart who will pressure you to spend the money for their benefit rather than yours. Some people among your friends and family may try to hit you up for a loan or a gift. And if you have an acquaintance who markets any type of financial investment instruments, he or she may be keeping an eye out for such opportunities to influence you to buy something from them that will put a nice commission in their pocket whether or not it benefits you.

If money tends to run through your hands faster than you would like it may be a good idea to use your insurance settlement to buy a Certificate of Deposit or a bond. This way the money will be tied up for a period of time in a safe place making it less tempting to spend impulsively. Talk with a banker in general terms about this so they will not steer you to make a purchase you do not want. Do your research so that you will be confident with your decision to make such a purchase.

Either way, park your money in a safe place until you are ready to buy another horse or spend the money on something else. Block out the background noise of others trying to influence you. You will know when you are ready. You decide how you want to spend the money.

CHAPTER 17

WILL YOUR HORSE GO TO HEAVEN?

I believe that horses do go to Heaven. And I base this on information from the Bible. Following the flood in Genesis, Chapter Eight, verse one talks about God remembering Noah, his family and all of the animals that were with them in the ark. And in Genesis Chapter Nine, verses 9 – 17 the Bible talks about God stating that He established a covenant with Noah, his descendants, and all of the animals with him. (A covenant is a vow or a promise, in this case made by God that He establishes forever, which He guarantees that He will not break.) In this covenant God said that He would not ever cause a flood again that would cut off all life on the earth.

God went on to say that He would put rainbows in the sky as a sign of His covenant to all living creatures, and whenever the rainbow appears, He would see it and remember that covenant. Three times in that biblical passage He talks about all living creatures being included in that covenant. As one of my college professors used to say, "all" means "all." And "all living creatures" includes horses. In the last part of that passage it says that the covenant, or agreement, is "everlasting." That means forever and according to God He will not cancel it or change His mind about it. In order to keep that covenant or promise, God must take horses to Heaven along with people and every other living creature. If horses are not included then He would have broken His covenant. That covenant still stands today.

The Bible talks about animals in Heaven as well as people. It talks about one Heaven. A lot of children have been told that their dog will go to Dog Heaven or their pony will go to Pony Heaven. I do not know where those thoughts originated. The Bible talks about one Heaven where we can all be together. The Bible talks about one Heaven where all people can choose to go.

And our horses will go to the same one and only Heaven that we will live in together forever.

In the last book of the Bible, Revelation, horses are directly discussed in the specific realm of Heaven. Revelation, Chapters 5 and 6, talks about the seven seals of a scroll being opened in Heaven. A white horse comes out of the first seal, a red horse comes out of the second, a black horse comes out of the third, and a pale horse comes out of the fourth. Revelation Chapter 5 states that the scroll with the seals is in God's right hand as He sits on the throne of Heaven. Revelation Chapter 19, verse 11, says that the author of that book of the Bible saw Heaven open before him and a white horse was standing there. From this biblical evidence, it seems clear that horses do go to Heaven. And that may ease the minds of some people who are grieving the loss of their horses.

Speaking of white horses, young and adult horses we see living and breathing that look like they are white are not genetically white. They have some pigmentation somewhere on their skin and/or have the dominant gene for the color gray. This pigmentation could only be a small area or spot of color on the horse. Gray horses are commonly born of any color and turn partly gray or dapple gray to fully gray, increasingly become completely white haired as they age.

Truly genetically white horses are conceived in the womb but they are either still born or die soon after birth. This happens because they are missing the ileum part of their small intestines. They are unable to completely process food. If they are born alive they colic and cannot live outside the womb for more than two days and are generally euthanized or die due to the pronounced pain. I remember a foal born at my college's barn that only had pigmentation at the very tip of her tail, indicating she had the ileum and therefore allowing her to live.

The Bible talks about white horses living in Heaven. This combined information says that yes, white horses are alive, but only in Heaven beyond the time of death between conception and up to two days after birth. That is further encouraging proof that horses of all colors do go to Heaven and we will see them again when we get there.

CHAPTER 18

BONDING WITH A NEW HORSE AFTER LOSING YOUR HORSE

Sometimes the transition to your new horse seems relatively fast and easy. Sometimes it takes a long time to bond with him after losing your horse. He has a different personality and feel under saddle. He will respond differently to training. And as you try to establish a connection with him your heart may ache for the horse you lost. As you go through the process of bonding with her you may feel pangs of guilt for betraying the memory of your favorite horse, especially when you realize that you are enjoying more and more days with your new horse. That is normal. Be patient with yourself. I cannot stress that enough. Have a good cry if you need to and know that it is okay to delight in your new horse.

Jane's Story

Jane came to me after she bought her new dressage horse Theo to replace the one she had lost to old age. Jane had lost Rusty after owning him for fourteen years. Jane had no children and Rusty had been the center of her life from the first time she rode him before she even bought him.

Jane told me she was having a difficult time bonding with Theo. She felt guilty about buying a new horse so soon after Rusty had died. It had been a year since Rusty died and eight months since she bought Theo. She really liked Theo but she could not allow herself to love him like she had loved Rusty. Theo was a perfect mount for her dressage competitions. He had a sweet disposition. There was nothing to dislike about him. It just hurt Jane to have Theo and not have Rusty anymore.

Jane and I talked about the grieving process and how it is okay to grieve Rusty. And it is perfectly fine to let herself grow to love Theo and establish the bond she wanted so desperately to have with him.

After we talked Jane decided to have her own private memorial for Rusty. She wrote a letter to him telling him how much she loved and missed him and that she wanted him to rest in peace. She bought a biodegradable helium balloon and went to the area of the farm where Rusty had been buried the previous year. Jane tied her letter to the balloon. She poured her heart out talking to Rusty. She released the balloon with the letter attached and watched it rise to Heaven. Then Jane wept. It was a turning point for her. She chose to make peace with Rusty's death. Then things began to change in her relationship with Theo. She gave herself permission to love him.

Weeks later I spoke with Jane again. She had a smile on her face. She felt closer to Theo and the bonding process between the two of them was going well. She found out that Theo loves her favorite candy so she shares that treat with him every time she sees him. And she enjoys riding him now. That does not mean she does not remember Rusty or experience occasional sadness over his death. She also smiles when she remembers some of the funny things that happened with Rusty, like when he always broke the lead rope when she tied him up outside his stall at the farm so she switched to using cross ties soon after she bought him.

Jane is happier and more relaxed now. She can go on with her new horse Theo and enjoy him and life again. And Jane is learning more about Theo and his personality since she gave herself permission to love him too. And she realized that Rusty would be okay if he knew she had another horse. It took some time and now life is better for both Theo and Jane.

CHAPTER 19

MEMORIES OF YOUR HORSE

Your memories of your horse are very important. Along with the sadness of losing your horse you probably have a lot of good and amusing memories. There were times when you felt like you were on top of the world with your horse when you achieved a goal – anything from mastering a lead change at home in your own private riding ring to winning at a big class at a prestigious horse show. There are times to remember that were very special such as relaxing after a ride and your horse putting his head on your shoulder. Each of us has multiple stories to tell that can help us get through the grieving process and enrich our lives beyond the special times we had with our horses.

Memorializing Your Horse

You may want to find a meaningful way to memorialize your horse. There is an infinite variety of ways to do that. Some ways can be very private and some ways can be public. It all depends on your own personal thoughts and feelings. You can spend as little or as much money as you want. You can decide when and under what circumstances. Your horse's life counted and still means a lot to you. How would you like to memorialize your horse? There is a list of suggestions next.

Ways to Memorialize Your Horse

The following is a list of ideas that you might use to memorialize your horse. You can choose from them and/or come up with your own unique ideas.

- You can do something as personal and private as sending up a balloon with a note to your horse like Jane.

- Several years ago I saw a horse's obituary in a four page full color ad in a national horse magazine. You could do something extravagant like that to show how much you loved your horse or choose a smaller section in a regional horse magazine or newsletter. Or choose something in between depending on how much money you want to spend.

- Establish a medical research fund for horses like Eva and Joe.

- Donate any amount of money to your favorite cause in your horse's name for research, a horse sanctuary, a veterinary scholarship, etc.

- You could foster or adopt another horse who needs a loving home temporarily or permanently.

- You can choose what to do with your horse's body after death. You could bury him on your farm or the farm where you boarded him. You could have her cremated like Brittany did with Jet and put her ashes in a special urn to either bury or keep in a place of honor.

- Organize a fundraising event to memorialize your horse like Eva and Joe.

- Fight for legislation to help find horses who are lost or stolen.

- Write an article or a book about your relationship with your horse.

- If you horse died in a fire you could donate money to your local fire department to help upgrade their equipment.

- Plant a shade tree in your paddock or pasture for future horses to enjoy.

- Sponsor a class at a horse show in memory of your horse.

- Hold a raffle at a horse show to raise funds for an organization that helps horses.

- Have a headstone or monument made for your horse.

- Plant flowers on your horse's grave site.

- Hire an artist to create a painting of your horse.

- Donate some of your horse's equipment to a therapeutic riding program.

- Create a quilt using different photos of your horse for each square or hire someone to make one for you.

- Donate containers of your horse's favorite treats to a horse sanctuary.

- Volunteer at a horse sanctuary or therapeutic riding program. This way you can share your love of horses with others.

There are a lot of ways to memorialize your horse. These are just suggestions that you can think about doing. This is the story about your life with your horse. Do what you want to do to remember your special horse.

CHAPTER 20

YOUR STORY

When you have lost your horse, you have your own unique story. The questions on the following pages of this chapter may help you work through some of your own grief. It can help you remember special times and feelings about your horse. Take your time and answer the questions when you are ready. Skip questions that you want to think about and answer them later. Or just leave them blank. There aren't any right or wrong answers. It is about you and your personal experience with your unique horse.

1. How are you dealing with the loss of your   horse?

2. What are some of your other thoughts and feelings about losing your horse?

3. In what ways do you feel differently from the time before you lost your horse?

4. What coping skills have you used in the past when you experienced a loss? How would they help you now?

5.   How are your relationships with friends and family as you go through this process? How do you feel about those relationships?

6.   Have you found people whom you trust that you can talk with about grieving the loss of your horse? Write their names or initials down here.

7. What would you like other people to know about what you are going through right now?

8. Who has been the most helpful and supportive to you? In what ways are they most helpful?

9. Have you written anything about your grieving experience in a journal? What is one story that you wrote down?

10. Has this been harder than you thought it would be? In what ways has it been harder?

11. Have you been through anything else difficult lately? Write down those things.

12. Some people find it difficult to eat or sleep when they have lost a special horse. Are you eating and sleeping okay?

13. Are you feeling overwhelmed now? What can you do to help yourself alleviate those feelings?

14. Are you getting back to some of your other activities that you enjoy? What are they? In what ways are they helping you?

15. What are some of your favorite memories of your horse?

16. What were your favorite activities with your horse?

17. What are some of the special things about your horse that made him or her special and unique?

18. What is your favorite story about something you experienced   with your horse?

19. Write about the funniest experience you ever had with your horse.

20. Would you like to either draw a picture of you horse or attach a copy of one of your favorite photos? You can also write down links to your favorite online pictures and videos of your horse.

21. How would you like to remember your horse?

22. How are you feeling about getting another horse? Would you like to wait or get another one right away? Would you like to postpone your decision for a while?

23. Find four things each day that are positive in your life to be thankful for and write them down in your journal or on sticky notes placed somewhere you can see to encourage you in your daily routine.

24. Be kind to yourself and give yourself grace. Ask yourself if you are doing or thinking anything at any given moment that is either harmful or helpful.

25. How would you like to memorialize your horse?

26. Write down any further notes about your horse and you that you would like to express. Again, there aren't any right or wrong answers. Take your time. This is about you, your horse and your story.

Conclusion

If you are ever in this situation you can take comfort from knowing that the process of grieving the loss of your horse is normal. And there is no set timeline or time limit. Your experience is your experience. You do not have to suffer alone. There are people who care about you during this difficult time. Find them and pour out your heart. People who care very deeply about you cannot know exactly how you feel no matter how hard they try. They can only care and be there for you. Please give them some grace.

Grieving is different for each person each time. It is okay to cry and to laugh over memories of your horse. And there is biblical evidence that horses do go to Heaven. So enjoy the horse you have as long as you can. Keep your special and heart-warming memories of previous horses and know that it is normal to grieve the loss of your horse and yet know that someday you will meet again in Heaven.

About the Author

Rebecca Crow has been coaching and mentoring people since 1989. She started her first job with horses at the age of thirteen and went on to start her first horse business in her twenties. After buying her first horse at age fourteen and participating in both 4-H Horse Projects and FFA Horse Judging Team Competitions, Rebecca went on to graduate with honors in Equine Science and Management from Diamond Oaks in Cincinnati, Ohio. After that she attended the Horse Production and Management Program at The Ohio State University. Rebecca graduated Summa Cum Laude in Psychology from Liberty University in Lynchburg, Virginia. Rebecca is a member of Psi Chi, the National Honor Society for Psychology. Rebecca's other education includes Riding

Instructor Training through Camp Horsemanship Association and Budget Counselor Training as well as Business By the Book Training through Crown Financial Ministries. Rebecca is a graduate of Professional Life Coaching, Caring for People God's Way, Health and Wellness Coaching, and Hope Coaching (for those going through the journey of cancer) and Caring for Kids God's Way through the American Association of Christian Counselors. Rebecca has experience cross-culturally coaching people from other countries, including France, Germany, Philippines, and Latin American countries.

Rebecca lives on a farm in the mountains of Alabama with her husband Tom, their dogs Abby, Jonah, Sadie and Skeeter, and their cats Josie, Patch Quilt and Ariel.

Rebecca M. Crow's Other Books

Available on Amazon.com

and through

other book retailers worldwide

Grieving the Loss of Your Pet: How to Survive Your Journey

Kindle and Print Editions

How to Save Time & Money with Your Horse Veterinarian:

Treat Your Horse Right!

An Interview with Marcia Thibeault, DVM

Kindle Edition

You may contact Rebecca through her email address:
beccacagle@juno.com

(Please put "Equestrian Life Coach" in the subject line)

Made in the USA
Middletown, DE
01 May 2023

29853382R00136